~ Ontario's Quiet Leader ~

JAMES NOBLE ALLAN

THE MAN · THE MASON · THE MPP

ALLISON F. GOWLING

tellwell

Tellwell Talent
www.tellwell.ca

ISBN
978-1-77302-188-1 (Paperback)
978-1-77302-189-8 (eBook)

TABLE OF CONTENTS

PREFACE

WE ARE NOW IN AN AGE WHERE MANNERS, CONSIDERATION, RESPECT FOR OTHERS AND their beliefs and opinions, which are especially seen in the "fishbowl" we know as the Ontario Legislature, are rarely used and seen even less. Some of us yearn for a return to a seemingly lost generation where everyone treated everybody with dignity, courtesy and respect. We knew our neighbours, and even everyone in town and people did not lock their doors at night.

I was born into that generation, the late 1950's and early and mid 1960's, in small-town, rural Ontario. This is where I remember some people who would be born, baptised, educated, work, marry, raise children and die, and who may not have traveled from their homes any more than 50 or 100 miles... (Remember, I was educated in the British Imperial system, and old habits are hard to break!).

It was a day where men holding doors for ladies was the rule, rather than the exception, where extremely few, if any businesses, were open on a Sunday and sports were rarely played on a Sunday. It was a day where men wore wide-brimmed fedoras, ladies were required to wear a hat when in a courtroom and the birth certificates of children who were born out of wedlock were stamped with the word "Illegitimate."

And let us not forget, when those of us who were old enough to be able to go to the liquor store, made out one of those 5" by 7" order forms with our names and what we wanted with the corresponding stock number, we then took it to the clerk, then paid for our purchase, while the clerk filled our order from the racks in the back of the store while we waited at the counter to pick up our acquisition.

And that clerk at the LCBO? He likely knew who you were, knew your parents, your siblings and likely when your birthday was.

James Noble Allan was an incredibly integral part of that long-ago society, he was Treasurer of Ontario, the right-hand man of "Old Man Ontario," Leslie Frost, who was another Brother in the Craft. Our Past Grand Master was a distinguished parliamentarian who worked all of the time for all of his constituents, not just those who voted for him and at election time.

Like so many of his time, James Noble Allan came from humble roots. He was a Haldimand County farm boy, to whom service to God, family, the church, and the community were first and foremost, and who was a great visionary who could well have been, if circumstances had unfolded in a different way, Premier of Ontario.

However, you likely know very little of James Allan, unless you are over 60, maybe 50, and are native to Haldimand County with your family roots going back for several generations.

I had the inspiration to write this book in a place that is most familiar and comfortable to me.

My wife and I were on a short holiday over the Easter weekend in April 2010, having driven to New Liskeard, ON with the express intent of burying ourselves in the Highway Bookshop, an tiny little used bookstore of some 500 000 books, on Highway #11, at the intersection of Highway #11B, six miles south of New Liskeard, ON, near Cobalt, ON. Unfortunately, due to the deaths of the owners and no buyers for the bookstore, this lovely place has since closed its doors.

While searching for my usual choice of reading: history, philosophy, biography and the like, I picked up a three volume set of the memoirs of John Diefenbaker, whom I knew was a Mason, and the memoirs of other great Canadian leaders, I was struck by the thought and realization that there had been nothing written, at least that I was aware of, on James Noble Allan.

By the time we had finished our exploration of the Highway Bookshop and having driven home with the trunk of the car filled with many boxes of books, I made the decision to research and write a book on James Allan.

While James Allan was a quiet, humble man who worked very hard for his family, his community, his constituents, his party and the Craft, he was also a "larger-than-life" person who played a very critical role in shaping modern-day Ontario. He was also a leader to the tens of thousands of Masons across Ontario.

Yet, in the little more than a generation that has passed since James Allan passed away, and the two generations that have gone by since James Allan last sat in the Ontario Legislature for Haldimand-Norfolk for 24 years, and the almost-three generations that have slid by since James Allan sat at the right-hand of Leslie Frost, John Robarts and William Davis, precious little is known by many people about this great man, parliamentarian and leader.

Researching, drafting and publishing this book have been a labour of love for me, and I am grateful for the assistance of the many people I have interviewed and the new people I have met and made friends with.

I hope to at least attempt to fill the literary void regarding James Allan, so that future generations will know who James Allan was, and not question why his name graces the Burlington Bay Skyway when they drive over it.

And I thank the Great Architect of the Universe for allowing me the occasion and this moment in time to compose this tome and to bring history to life.

So mote it be.

W. Bro. Allison Gowling
May 2016
Jarvis, ON

INTRODUCTION BY THE HONOURABLE BRO. WILLIAM GRENVILLE DAVIS

I AM BOTH PLEASED AND HONOURED TO HAVE BEEN ASKED BY THE AUTHOR, W. BRO. ALLISON Gowling, to write an introduction for this book on my brother Mason, my friend, fellow parliamentarian and cabinet minister, James Noble Allan, or as he preferred to just be called, "Jim."

It was an honour to work with Jim for over 15 years in the Legislature and in the provincial cabinet, and for many years afterwards.

Jim was an icon in his time and his influence on provincial policies and initiatives are still seen and felt in the over 40 years after Jim left the Legislature.

To see one example of Jim's lasting legacy, one only has to drive on the QEW between Toronto and the east end of Hamilton. It was Jim's manoeuvring and foresight that brought us the Burlington Bay James N. Allan Skyway, from a dream, to a real plan, onto construction and use.

And it was Jim's financial prowess as Treasurer that laid the groundwork for, and made possible the many projects that the Frost and Robarts' governments and mine as well, undertook on behalf of Ontarians.

Jim was also very involved with the Niagara Parks Region development.

Jim was not only a leader as well, but a giant among the men of his time, to use a time-worn phrase, who had the vision, the ability and the wherewithal to not only know where he wanted to go, but was able to take himself, and the Province of Ontario, there to the benefit of both.

Jim came to Queen's Park at age 57, which has been a time when most people start turning their thoughts to retirement, not taking on a larger occupation.

From 1963 to 1967, while Jim was still Treasurer, he was the Deputy Grand Master, then the Grand Master of the Grand Lodge of Canada in the Province of Ontario. Jim's boundless energy, even into his late 60's and early 70's, had always amazed me and everyone else in our caucus.

Although Jim stepped away from the Treasurer's job in 1966 to devote more time for his position of Grand Master of the Grand Lodge of Canada in the Province of Ontario, he remained in cabinet as Minister without portfolio. I used to joke with Jim that he went into "semi-retirement."

When Jim had to leave the Legislature in 1975 after he failed to retain his seat in that general election, he was very much missed by everyone.

I was fortunate enough to be able to keep in touch reasonably well with Jim for the next 18 years.

Many thanks to W. Bro. Allison Gowling for bringing this story of Jim Allan, not only to the generation that remembers him fondly, but to those generations who do not know him but should.

The Honourable, and Bro., William Grenville Davis
Brampton, ON
May 2016

WITH MANY THANKS TO...

I WANT TO TAKE THIS OPPORTUNITY TO THANK THE PEOPLE WHO HELPED ME FORMULATE this book. I give many thanks to those persons who gave assistance, gave willingly of their time to share their memories of, and writings about, James Allan and to provide support.

- My wife Annemiek, who has steadfastly stood by me with her unwavering support, her help and (sometimes) sage (and usually unwanted) advice for 35-plus years (and you people say I am nuts???);
- My two adoring (yeah...suuuuuuure...) children, Gregory and Kyle for following me in the Craft and for staying out of my way while I was writing this book;
- Ian Durand and the other volunteers of the Dunnville District Heritage Association;
- The late Lorne Sorge of the Dunnville Chronicle;
- R. W. Bro. Doug Madill;
- The late R. W. Bro. Harry Bartlett;
- The late V. W. Bro. Arthur Bradford;
- R. W. Bro. Paul Shaver;

- V. W. Bro. Michael Palmer;
- V. W. Bro. John Chapman;
- W. Bro. John Hart Sr. and Bro. John Hart Jr.;
- M. W. Bro. Terrance Shand;
- M. W. Bro. John C. Greene;
- The staff at the offices of the Grand Lodge of Canada in the Province of Ontario;
- The Honourable, and Bro. William G. Davis;
- The Honourable, and Bro. Robert F. Nixon;
- The Honourable Darcy McKeough;
- Neil Paul for his masterful (and brutal) editing of this book and for his critique;
- The late R. W. Bro. Keith Cosier, who was a friend, a mentor, a sounding board and most of all, a true brother;
- My parents, Norman and Ethel Gowling, for instilling me with those rural Methodist values that have assisted me in life and with writing this tome.
- And many thanks to Bonnie Unrau for her taking the time out of her generous teacher pension-funded retirement to read my book and write several very nice reviews for the local newspapers.

CHAPTER 1

"THE START OF THE BEGINNING"

IT WAS LIKELY A USUAL DAY IN THE MIDDLE OF NOVEMBER, THE LEAVES HAD FALLEN AND have been raked perhaps, there is probably quite a chill in the air, the kind of frostiness that just permeates your bones deep enough to remind you that winter, and snow, are just around the corner.

The road in front of the farm that James Allan's father owns and works what we now know as the King's Highway #3, is just a bumpy and rutted dirt road, known to everyone then as the Talbot Road.

Talbot Road was named after Colonel John Talbot, who headed up a force of militia that was significant in helping the British defend the Niagara Peninsula in the War of 1812 against the Americans. Colonel Talbot's troops and militia blazed and built the original Talbot Road through the thick bush so that troops and militia from the eastern end of the

Niagara Peninsula could reach at Fort Detroit quickly when needed. That route was only 265 miles on foot, or horseback if you were lucky enough to have a horse.

On 13 November 1894, on the outskirts of the Village of Canborough, in Canborough Township, in Haldimand County, on the dairy farm that fronted on the Talbot Road on the eastern outskirts of the hamlet of Canborough, the only child, an infant named James Noble Allan, was born to James Allan and Minerva Janet Allan, nee Swayze. Minerva was born on that same farm on Talbot Road in 1857 and passed away in 1933.

It is noteworthy that James Allan's father was 54 when he was born and this would later prove significant in the younger James' later years. James passed away in 1931, and both James' father and Minerva lay at rest in the Canborough Cemetery on County Road #63 just a bit east of the old Canborough Baptist Church.

James' father was first married to Martha Allan, who was born in 1842, but Martha passed away in March 1885, shortly after giving birth to a daughter, also named Martha.

That infant Martha died at the age of five months in August 1885.

James' father and his first wife, Martha, also had a daughter, Lottie, who was born in 1881 and later married Thomas Hedley of Canfield and passed away in 1967. Lottie is interred at the Canfield Cemetery.

There is a gravestone in the Canborough Cemetery for a Florence Allan who was born in 1870 and passed away in 1934. Whether Florence was a half-sister to James is unclear at present. Research of the remaining records of the former Canborough Methodist (now United) Church proved sketchy, at best.

James' father later married Minerva Swayze sometime between 1890 to 1894, and James may have been the only child of that union. The author could not locate any marriage records of Canborough Methodist (United) Church.

It merits mentioning that this author attempted to further research into the marriages, births, baptismal and deaths of James' father, his two wives, Martha and Minerva and their children.

Unfortunately however this author has had difficulty in accessing the necessary church records in Canborough Methodist (later United) Church.

At the time of James' birth, Canborough Methodist Church was one point of a three-point charge with the Moote Methodist Church on Moote Road off the Robinson Road near Dunnville and Bethel Methodist Church in Attercliffe Station.

In later years, after the Moote Methodist Church closed and Bethel Methodist Church became part of another multi-point charge, Canborough Methodist (by that time, United) Church was paired with the Canfield United Church in a two-point charge until Canborough United Church closed some 10 years ago.

This author has attempted to track the Allan family through Canborough Methodist Church records, but he found that all of the records of Canborough United Church, which were expected to be kept at Canfield United Church as that was where the ministers of the day had their Church office, were not accessible.

The records of Canborough United Church at Canfield were incomplete. This author was only able to peruse some basic church records, since there were no separate ledgers of births, baptisms, marriages or deaths.

Mind you, this was common at the time. The accuracy and completeness of church records fell completely upon the pastor of the time. And like all walks and in all professions of life, not every pastor could be as diligent or as meticulous as their successor or predecessor. With a pastor having a three-point charge, as was the case with Canborough, Moote and Bethel, a large, if not huge, number of parishioners and families that would require ongoing pastoral care. The area would have been spread over a fairly large locale, somewhere in the area of 50 to 75 square miles. Paperwork, such as record keeping, would be the first to suffer if the pastor had many constraints and demands upon his time.

As this author's mother used to say, there are only 24 hours in a day...and sometimes you think you may need at times 36 hours in a day in order to get everything done.

Pastoral care required travel that had to be undertaken by horse or horse and buggy. Needless to say, travel by horse or horse and buggy is not the swiftest mode of travel, but it was the only mode of travel available at that time as the nearest railroads were either in Canfield, Dunnville or Smithville. These were of no use in this type of circumstances.

The distance from Canborough Methodist Church to the Moote Road Methodist Church would have been about two miles to two-and-one half miles. The distance from the Moote Road Methodist Church to the Bethel Methodist Church would have been about the same. And the distance from the Moote Road Methodist Church back to Canborough Methodist Church would have been about four miles.[1]

No matter how you measure, a Methodist preacher in 1890's Ontario with a three-point charge would have his travel cut out for him.

Also at that time, when a church closed, the church records usually went into the attic of a member of that church, rather than into a proper archive, which in all likelihood at that time, did not exist. There those records would languish for years, decades, generations or even several generations, before being stumbled upon.

A prime example of such is the former Presbyterian Church in Canfield.

This Presbyterian Church was located in the easternmost corner of Lot 7, North Half, Concession 1 in North Cayuga. This particular lot was the farm that this author's grandparents, Fred and Flossie Gowling and later his parents, Norman and Ethel Gowling, owned and worked for several generations.[1]

This author recalls his mother telling him years ago that the Presbyterian Church had closed, due to declining membership, in 1890 and the remaining members went a half-mile west to the Canfield Methodist Church.

The church records went into someone's attic for safe keeping and there they sat for over 100 years.

This author had been told by many people that several persons were recently looking for those old records for decades, to no avail. But someone, whose descendants had been members of the old Canfield Presbyterian Church, happened to stumble onto those church records in their attic when searching for something else about five years ago.

If that person had been looking specifically for those records, they would have never found them. However, since that person was looking for something else instead of those records, those old church records virtually jumped out in front of them.

This is Murphy's Law at its best.

At the time of James' birth, Sir John Thompson was the Prime Minister of Canada; Sir Oliver Mowat was the Premier of Ontario and Ontario was an almost totally agricultural-based economy and society, especially in Haldimand County.

This was a day when only the homes of the well-to-do had electricity and/or running water, the remainder read or worked by the light of candles or a kerosene lamp. Water for daily use was drawn from a nearby well, or if you were fortunate, you had a cast iron pump at the well. Or if you were a farm wife who was exceedingly providential, you would have had a cast iron pump mounted on your kitchen counter and hooked up to your well. This author recalls such a pump in his parents' kitchen in the early 1960's.

What was also the norm was that farm work, such as milking, feeding livestock, etc., was done by hand. However, while some field work at that time was beginning to see the future with mechanization, such as grain threshing, there was still a great deal of manual work that accompanied this age of early mechanization. Those sheaves of grain did not cut and stook themselves, then walk to the threshing machine, you know.

And the hay you fed your livestock was not baled into small, square bales or the huge round or rectangular bales you see today in the fields. You pitched it loose onto the wagon, hauled that dray with your team to the barn, you then raised your hay, one loose bundle at a time, from that cart to loft by way of your hay claw with a block and tackle. The hay did not walk or climb up into the loft either.

Once a young child like Jim Allan was deemed old enough to work and help around the farm, he would have been assigned work or chores suitable for his age and size. Responsibilities such as feeding and watering animals, mucking the stables and chicken pens out, throwing down hay for feed or straw for bedding from the mow, gathering eggs and the like, were standard procedures.

Everyone living on a farm in Ontario 100 or 125 years ago would pitch in, from the very young to the elderly, everyone working at tasks suitable to their age and abilities.

And in Haldimand County, up to 1951, property owners were also expected to grade the road that ran in front of their property as part of the property taxes. This author recalls going through the six or eight very large boxes of family papers, etc. and coming across a Haldimand County property tax bill from 1917 for $5.21. And printed across the bottom of the property tax bill was the statement; "Please remember to grade your road!"

It was the day where children, when they grew older, were expected to remain on the family farm and take over when their parents were no longer able to. Or the children could strike out on their own and purchase an existing farm nearby and work in conjunction with their parents.

It would be a rare occasion that any of a farmer's children would finish high school, or their "matriculation," let alone undertake a post-secondary education.

James Noble Allan was that exception.

In the coming chapters, the author will relate how the life of James Allan progressed and how James became not only one of the most influential persons and politicians of his generation, but for the several other generations that would follow.

As well, James Allan would go on to become a leader and a role model for many members of a fraternity that dates itself to the building of King Solomon's Temple in Jerusalem.

And finally, but not in the least, James Allan was known and revered for being dedicated to God, to his church, to his family, to his fraternity and to his community.

CHAPTER 2
THE EARLY YEARS

WHEN JIM ALLAN WAS NEARING HIS SIXTH BIRTHDAY IN SEPTEMBER 1899, HE WOULD HAVE been sent off to the quintessential one-room schoolhouse that served his family's school section or area.

Unlike today, schools 100 years ago were laid out in what were called "school sections," and one-room schoolhouses were constructed in such a geographical manner that those schools were located within a reasonable walking distance to and from the homes for all students in that section.

The one-room schoolhouse that James Allan attended would have been likely a walk of one mile, or a mile-and-a-half, perhaps two miles at most, as this was the system that Egerton Ryerson designed. Our present-day system still encompasses much of what Egerton Ryerson planned nearly a century-and-a-half ago.

However, as was the norm in an agrarian-based society like Ontario 100, 150 or more years ago, children were let out of school near the end of June, perhaps earlier. During the late spring, summer and early autumn, those children would assist their parents on the family farm with the bringing in hay and harvesting crops, such as wheat, oats, barley, rye, etc, not to mention any barn cleaning, manure spreading, repairs or construction.

James Allan would have been no exception to that rule.

James Allan would have continued to attend that one-room schoolhouse until he had finished what is now Grade 7 or 8. However, the next step for James Allan's, or most children's education normally would have been for James to find his way to Dunnville to finish his "matriculation" at the local school that served the town of Dunnville, or what we call secondary school now.

To do so would have involved a trek that may have entailed catching a ride with a neighbour, or hitchhiking or even walking the almost nine miles to the High School at Dunnville. The nearest station and train that would take you into Dunnville proper was in Canfield, known at the time as the Buffalo & Lake Huron, the precursor to the Grand Trunk and later Canadian National Railway. However, Canfield was some six miles away to the west on the Talbot Road, in the opposite direction.

James Allan proved himself quite precocious in the one-room schoolhouse and was a most able student. So much so that in 1908, nearing the age of 14, James Allan was accepted as a student at the Ontario Agricultural College in Guelph, which was the forerunner of the University of Guelph.

Even today, it is rarely heard that a child of 14 or 15 years old who is accepted into a post-secondary institution.

As it was then, and as it is now, your church was an important part of the community. And Canborough was no different than any other small Ontario town, village or hamlet.

A hamlet such as Canborough, like Canfield six miles to the west on Talbot Road, had more than one church. The Church the Allans were members of was then the Canborough Methodist Church, which in 1926, like the Canfield Methodist Church became part of the new United Church of Canada.

Canborough also had a Baptist Church, which was located less than 100 yards from the Methodist Church.

The Baptist Church closed in 1963 and was vacant for a number of years, then was converted to the Jubilee Faith Centre. About 2000, the Jubilee Faith Centre re-located to the former Canborough Central School, some six to seven miles up the Talbot Road, now the King's Highway #3. The former Canborough Baptist Church now sits empty and idle again.

As mentioned in Chapter 1, James' father was 54 when James was born, and his father wanted him to have a head start in education and in life.

As with most of the students of James Allan's day, when James Allan finished his education, he was expected to take his place on the family farm beside his parents.

However, James Allan was not your usual student. James was to embark, just eight years into "Canada's century" as stated by Sir Wilfrid Laurier, on an education, then later a business career, later municipal politics and then into the Ontario Legislature and an illustrious Masonic career. In that time period, shortly before the Great War through to his passing in 1992, James Noble Allan was a household name in not only Haldimand and Norfolk Counties, but all over Ontario. James likely knew you too, as well as your parents, your siblings, your grandparents, your children and likely all of your neighbours.

And he probably even knew your dog's name as well.

There were heady days ahead for James Allan.

CHAPTER 3
OFF TO COLLEGE

IT IS THE LATE SUMMER OF 1908 AND JAMES ALLAN IS APPROACHING THE AGE OF 14 YEARS. He has finished his elementary education, but at his father's urging, James is eschewing his "matriculation" or high school education in Dunnville and has been accepted into the Bachelor of Agricultural Program at the Ontario Agricultural College at Guelph, ON.

James Allan is now able to do what very few of his peers could, or would be able to do, and that is attend a post-secondary institution with his acceptance at the Ontario Agricultural College at Guelph, which was the forerunner of today's University of Guelph.

Remember, these are the days long before OSAP Student Loans. You, or your parents, had to foot the entire bill for any post-secondary education; tuition, books, room and board. And let us not forget travel to and from Guelph.

This was a distance of some 61 miles, or almost 100 kilometres, one way. The roads in not only Haldimand County, but adjoining and other counties, such as Wentworth, Halton and Wellington Counties, were not much better than Haldimand County's roads. The King's Highway system did not come into existence until 1917 and Highway #3 and Highway #6 not until 1920.

So, if James Allan wanted to go to Guelph, he had to catch a ride with a friend or neighbour to Guelph, or he had to hitchhike there. Or he had to find his way to Canfield, the nearest Grand Trunk terminal, catch the daily mixed train to Caledonia, switch again to take the mixed train to Hamilton and then switch again to take the train to Guelph.

While the cost of a one-way train fare to Guelph would be approximately perhaps $1.50 to $2.00, which may seem minuscule to us today. In 1912, $2.00 may have been a week's wages for a labourer, or the cost of a ladies' dress from the archetypal Eaton's catalogue, even a month's room and board for a college student. Two dollars was a considerable sum in 1908 and not to be spent unwisely

Please realize that the average farm income in 1908 in Canada was about $9 000 per annum.[2] So possibly, many of those farming incomes in a rather hardscrabble area such as Haldimand County could well likely be much, much lower. Now, remember a farm couple could grow and can their own vegetables and fruit, bake their own bread, butcher and smoke their own meat (a freezer was a luxury virtually unheard of in 1908 to a farmer), and heat their homes with wood cut on their own property. So a farming income of $1 000 to $2 000, or even less, per annum is within the realm of possibility in Haldimand County in 1908.

This author was able to obtain, from the University of Guelph's Archival and Special Collections Department, the tuition costs for OAC students for the years from 1908 to 1914 for the OAC.

As you will note, the then-OAC changed its tuition structure between the 1908/1909 and 1909/1910 academic years, but remained consistent after that.

Tuition for 1908/1909 was $16.00 per year for resident students and $40 per year for non-resident students.

Tuition for 1909-1910: $20.00 per year for First and Second Year students from Ontario; $50.00 per year for Third and Fourth Year students from Ontario. Tuition was $50.00 per year for students from provinces other than Ontario, including Newfoundland. Tuition was $100.00 per year for students outside of Canada and Newfoundland.

The tuition costs for the subsequent academic years of 1910/1911, 1911/1912, 1912/1913 and 1913/1914 were the same as the 1909/1910 academic year.[3]

However, along with the cost of James' tuition was cost of textbooks and room and board.

While there was no OSAP, there were on-campus student residences. Or you could find your own lodgings, hopefully a short walk to the College as the City of Guelph in 1908 only had two urban street car lines, one east-west and one north-south. A daily commute to and from Guelph and Dunnville was certainly not an option in the time prior to the Great War.

James Allan was able to live in the College's on-campus residences and the total cost of his first year of College was $150.00.[4]

Now it is not known if James Allan would have travelled home every weekend, as many post-secondary students do now, whether or not the parents want them to.

When one factors in the cost of travelling between home and Guelph, it is likely that James Allan, along with most of the College's students, would have gone only for one, maybe two, weekends a semester. Perhaps travel to home for Thanksgiving and another weekend? Then home for the Christmas Break and back to school after New Year's Day.

In order for James to get his Bachelor of Agricultural Science, James attended the Guelph OAC for six years.

While James Allan was attending OAC in Guelph, he met a young man and struck up a friendship with him. That young man was the son of a dairy farmer from St. George, ON who was some two-and-one-half years older than James. The amity that the two men struck up would last for more than 50 years.

When the two met, neither realized that some 40 years later they would spend the next 10 years facing each other across the floor of the Ontario Legislature, James Allan would be a backbencher and later a cabinet mainstay of Leslie Frost's Ontario Conservative government and Harry Nixon was be a member of the Ontario Legislature since 1919, a respected bastion of her Majesty's Loyal Opposition, the Ontario Liberal Party and a former Premier of Ontario.

James Allan would have known what a great gift and opportunity he had been given with his chance to attend the Ontario Agricultural College in Guelph. James was determined to make the most of this prospect, in all aspects possible.

CHAPTER 4
COMING HOME & MOVING FORWARD

IT IS THE SPRING OF 1914 AND JAMES ALLAN IS 19 AND HAS GRADUATED FROM THE ONTARIO Agricultural College in Guelph with a BSA, or Bachelor of Science - Agriculture.

James Allan, as expected returns to the family farm on Talbot Road on the edge of Canborough and begins to work alongside his father on the family farm. However, James Allan also had his eyes on other projects.

In those exhilarating days of an economic boom, before the horrors and carnage of the Great War that forever changed the lives of everyone in that generation, even the agricultural economy of Haldimand County, was growing at a great rate. Haldimand County farmers had difficulty in getting their products, produce, etc. to market.

At that time, the network of roads in Haldimand County, like many of its municipal counterparts was poor at best, as the

King's Highway #3 did not come into existence until 1920 and virtually all roads were dirt, maybe some were gravel, as paved roads were practically unheard of.

At that time, the only railroad lines in Haldimand County were the Buffalo & Lake Huron, later absorbed into the Grand Trunk system in 1881, the first railway line that ran through Haldimand County which was the second railway line constructed in Upper Canada in 1853 which ran north-west from Fort Erie, through Dunnville, Canfield and Caledonia onto Brantford, Stratford to its terminus in Goderich. Along with Buffalo & Lake Huron Railway, the Canada Southern, constructed in 1878, ran westward from Fort Erie to Windsor, through Canfield Junction and Hagersville. The Great Western Airline, which had been built in 1874, which by that time had become a part of the Grand Trunk system and also ran west from Welland to just outside St. Thomas at Yarmouth, and ran through Canfield Junction, Cayuga, Nelles Corners and Jarvis. There was also a TH&B spur that ran from the CPR line from Smithville, across Oswego Creek, through Dunnville and onto Port Maitland, but this was not built until about 1916.

So, unless you lived within a few miles of where these railroads passed, a farmer had difficulty in shipping his product to a market.

This was especially thorny if you were a dairy farmer. You had to get your milk to a dairy quickly. If you were shipping in winter and you were not fast enough, your milk would freeze; if it were spring, summer or fall, and you were not quick enough, Your milk would rapidly spoil without some form of refrigeration.

James Allan recognized that a service that would pick up raw milk from farmers and deliver it to a dairy was a service that was in great need for a large rural area such as Haldimand County.

Sometime during 1919 at the urging of an unknown local Canborough cheese maker, James Allan, in partnership with William Harvie, purchased the existing King Edward Creamery in Dunnville, which had been in business since the early 1900's. In a short time, the King Edward Creamery became known as the "Dunnville Dairy," and later, in 1959, as Puritan Dairy Products Limited.

In 1928, William Harvie sold his share of the creamery and went into the insurance business. James oversaw the creamery operations on his own until his election to the Ontario Legislature and when his various provincial, constituency and later cabinet duties required him to delegate the majority of the operation of the creamery to his son, J. Harvie Allan and his son-in-law, A. G. Sabiston.

In short course, the Dunnville Dairy started picking up raw milk from area farmers and delivering that milk to nearby dairies. James Allan was able to bring in raw milk, fresh eggs and such to the Dunnville Dairy's set-up on Chestnut Street where it ran into South Cayuga Street, almost directly across the street from the old Grand Trunk Railway station. From there, the Dunnville Dairy was able to ship their finished products all over Ontario and later into the United States.

By the 1940's, the Dunnville Dairy was not only picking up raw milk for processing, but eggs as well. The Dairy was producing and shipping to various retailers' fresh milk, butter, cheese, milk powder, ice delivery and ice cream. The Dunnville Dairy even had a storefront operation where it sold its products, and children loved the fresh, "Smooth As Velvet" ice cream.

The Dunnville Dairy was a major employer in the Dunnville area, requiring considerable manpower to operate the creamery, the retail store and to man the Dairy's fleet of trucks that were utilized for pickup and delivery of raw material and finished products.

James was known for being extremely loyal, fair and generous to his employees as James recognized that a workforce that was well-compensated and rewarded was a workforce that loyal to the end in return.

This treatment of employees today has unfortunately become almost non-existent. Most employers, or so it seems, believe loyalty is a one-way street, in only their direction.

Over the next 50 or so years, the Dunnville Dairy served many dairy farmers in the eastern end of Haldimand County by picking up their raw milk, delivering it to the dairy in Dunnville, processing, pasteurizing and bottling the milk and shipping it out to retailers all over Southwestern Ontario. If you are lucky, you can still pick up an old "Dunnville Dairy" milk bottle today on eBay or Kijiji.

However, during the 1960's, when James was not only very busy as an MPP and cabinet minister but also moving up the rungs the Grand Lodge in the Province of Ontario, James sold the Dunnville Dairy to Avondale in Beamsville. Unfortunately shortly after the Dunnville Dairy was sold, it was closed down.

Later, in 1974 the Dairy's interests were sold again to a Mississauga company who only seemed to want to acquire the name and any other valuable assets. The Dairy never operated again.

The building the Dunnville Dairy was housed in remained empty and left to deteriorate.

After a fire in 1991, the Dunnville Dairy building sat derelict until most of the remaining structure was torn down. A remainder of the Dairy building was rebuilt and integrated as part of a condominium complex in the late 1990's.[5]

Also, James Allan had settling down on his mind as well.

Back in his OAC days at Guelph, James Allan had met a young lady named Lilian Harvie of Orillia who was enrolled at the MacDonald Institute, which was attached to the OAC at Guelph.

The MacDonald Institute specialized in giving young ladies a university-style education in domestic services.

James and Lilian met at an OAC student dance that James Allan and Harry Nixon had helped organize, and their romance blossomed. Their engagement was announced in the Orilla Packet[6] and in August 1916 the two were married at Lilian's parents ' home in Orillia and James and Lillian settled on the family farm on Talbot Road in Canborough.

On 6 November 1919, a son named James Harvie Allan was born, and a sister, Lillian, followed shortly after.

As well, a part of James Allan's upbringing was also service to one's community.

James applied to join the Dunnville Lions Club and was of its most ardent and busiest members, being a part of the Lions community in Dunnville for over 30 years.

Also, James applied to join the Masonic Lodge in Dunnville, Amity Lodge No. 32. James was initiated into Masonry at the age of 23 on 12 June 1918, passed to the Second Degree on 18 December 1918 and raised to the Sublime Degree of a Master Mason on 2 February 1919.

James showed his prowess with the "Work," and worked his way through the chairs at Amity Lodge, and in 1925 was installed as Worshipful Master in the Chair of King Solomon at Amity Lodge #32 of the Grand Lodge of Canada in the Province of Ontario.

At the Annual Communication of Grand Lodge in Toronto on 17 July 1931, James Allan was elected to the Grand Lodge of Canada in the Province of Ontario as the District Deputy Grand Master for the Niagara District "A." James had as his District Secretary a local lawyer, Walter Robb, who later went on to be the District Deputy Grand Master for the Niagara District "A" in 1939, was later appointed to the bench and later on James Allan had R. W. Bro. Walter Robb appointed the head of the Liquor Control Board of Ontario.

This was the start of a Masonic career that would help make James Allan a very familiar name to Masons and their families throughout Ontario for many years to come.

CHAPTER 5

HELPING TO SHAPE HALDIMAND COUNTY

AS STATED IN AN EARLIER CHAPTER, ANY PERSON OF RURAL HERITAGE, MALE OR FEMALE has it drummed into them from birth that, after God, your church, your family, service to your neighbours and your community comes first and foremost. If this author may, to purloin a phrase from Rotary, service above self.

That vein of service ran deep in James Allan, and in 1915 at the politically tender age of 21, James Allan ran, and was elected to the Canborough Township Council. Over the next 36 years, James progressed, not only in municipal experience, but also in local popularity and James became the Reeve of Canborough Township. That experience and popularity would later propel James to become the Mayor of Dunnville and then James went on to be the Warden of Haldimand County.

One of James' preferred areas of focus was to improve the condition of the roads in, around and within Haldimand County.

Please remember what has been written in earlier chapters, property owners were expected, until 1951 under County by-laws, to grade and maintain the roads that fronted on their property. This author's grand-father's, and later his parents' farm was no exception to that expectation. There was a horse-drawn grader and blade that the author's father converted from horse-drawn to tractor-drawn in 1945 after this author's father had bought a brand-new 1945 McCormick-Deering Farmall "A" tractor.

The requirement for property owners having to grade the roads that fronted on your property was discontinued in 1951. After that, the grader was relegated to a fence line in our prover-bial "back forty" until it was dug out, hauled back up to the house and sold at the author's mother's farm auction in April 1973.

Upgrading County roads was no small effort as Haldimand County at that time was one of the largest counties in Ontario. In 1921, the only paved road was the newly-minted King's Highway #3, and that was only in paved in sections, the remaining sections being gravel and which had been designated as a King's Highway in 1920. However, the "new" King's Highway #3 was a far cry from what we drive on today.

In the days before, and after the Great War, and before World War II, most of the County and concession roads were dirt roads, rutted and uneven, with a few being gravel. With the spring thaw and rains and the fall wet season, Haldimand County's roads would be a quagmire, especially with our famous Haldimand clay. In the winter, those ruts would be frozen solid and driving a team and wagon, or your family's Model T Ford over these frozen runnels would be akin to driving over a lava field in which the flow had long since cooled and hardened into basalt.

However, while the 10 townships that made up Haldimand County and made it one of the largest, if not the largest, municipality in Ontario at that time, it did not mean that Haldimand County was one of the wealthiest.

In fact, with Haldimand County's economy almost 100 per cent agricultural-based at that time, it is likely Haldimand County would have been somewhere in the bottom third of counties in Ontario in regards to wealth. So James Allan would have had a very difficult time in raising funds for road repairs and capital improvements from property taxes in 1915 for Haldimand County. The province did not put in matching funds like they do today.

In the Haldimand County's "urban" areas, such as Dunnville, Caledonia, Hagersville, Cayuga and Jarvis, you would be very fortunate if the main streets, such as King's Highways #6 and #3 were paved. What we now know as King's Highway #54, which would be Caithness Street in Caledonia and Munsee Street in Cayuga, did not come into existence until 1937. The surrounding side streets would be dirt, or if the town was fortunate, those side streets would be topped with gravel...maybe.

And sidewalks? Sidewalks, if there were any at that time, were likely constructed of rough-hewn wooden planks nailed to runners and laid down between the buildings and the edge of the street. The location of any sidewalks would have been restricted to the main streets of any village or town. If you lived on a side street, you were very likely out of luck if you were walking along the side of the road.

There was the story that, when the Hamilton & Lake Erie Railway was planning its route from Hamilton to Jarvis, and later to Port Dover in the early 1850's, the Town of Caledonia pledged 20 000 pounds, over $40 000 in 1853 dollars, to secure the railway's route through Caledonia.

It is said that this huge expenditure to the railroad delayed proper sidewalks in Caledonia by some 20 years.

The Hamilton & Lake Erie Railway was not built until 1873, 20 years after the railway had been given the 20 000 pounds.

If you were a pedestrian in these areas, you were taking your life into your hands walking on those decrepit sidewalks, and even more so if you tried to cross the street.

While the automobile had become reasonably commonplace on some Ontario roads by 1915, in Haldimand County teams of horses pulling various types of wagons along Ontario's highways and Haldimand County's roads would have been the rule rather than the exception.

While there were the railroads that traveled through Haldimand County, you still had to get what you wanted to ship by rail to the railroad station. That meant you had to use the highway or the County roads to get to the railroad station.

It is noteworthy that the east end of Haldimand County, when it came to railroads, was under-serviced when compared to the middle and western sections of Haldimand County.

While Dunnville had two railway lines, only the Grand Trunk was a major line as the TH&B spur was a very light track and not built until about 1916, a small town like Canfield, due to the railroads choice of routes, had three major railway lines and stations in town or nearby, while slightly larger towns such as Cayuga, Caledonia, Hagersville and Jarvis had two railway lines.

Both Caledonia and Jarvis had two lines and a "Union" station while Hagersville had two lines and two stations.

However, Dunnville only had only one major line and a station, later with a short spur and a small station connecting Dunnville with the TH&B and CPR to the north-east.

Between 1915, when James Allan was first elected to Canborough Town Council and when James was elected to the Ontario Legislature as the MPP for Haldimand-Norfolk in 1951, James Allan moved from Township Councillor to Township Reeve, which is the equivalent of Mayor, of Canborough Township to Mayor of Dunnville and then onto Warden of Haldimand County.

One of James' lifelong friends and Masonic brother, the late V. W. Bro. Art Bradford, remembered James as a Township Councillor, Reeve, Mayor and Warden. He recalled that James was very hard working and had a penchant for making things happen as well as being very community minded. James was good for any cause in Canborough Township and was always involved "up to his eyeballs," and that was the only way James wanted it.

Art recalled that James was the driving force behind Canborough Township's Centennial Project for 1967, a new community centre, fire hall, community plaques and town square cairn, and James backed all of these projects fully. What also greatly assisted with the Township's Centennial Project, along with other Haldimand County-related issues and projects, was James's close association and friendship with then-Prime Minister Lester Pearson.

What impressed Art the most about James was his compassion for his fellow man. Art told me that, on many, many occasions, James would personally pay the hospital and medical bills of his friends, fellow church parishioners, Lion members and Amity brethren.

Remember, these were the days long before the Ontario Health Insurance Plan. One had to pay the doctors, the hospital and the pharmacy out of one's own pocket.

This author recalls, seeing a bill when sorting through some six or eight boxes of family papers, photographs, etc. the author "inherited" after the author's mother had moved. The author came across a bill from the Hamilton General Hospital for the Author's father's appendectomy at age 12. The bill for his father's surgery and hospital stay came to $28.00.

Art also remembered that James had a habit at the beginning of a speech, whether it was a political discourse or a Masonic dialogue, of always complimenting the ladies in attendance.

All the way along James Allan's municipal career, James developed an incredible reputation for making sure the issues, problems, needs, questions, etc. of his constituents, whether those citizens had voted for him or not, were taken care of properly.

As well during this time, James also worked as a part-time temporary Agricultural Representative, or "Ag Rep," for the Ontario Ministry of Agriculture, serving the farmers and agricultural sector of both Wentworth County, which is the Hamilton area, and Lanark County, which was north-west of Peterborough.

James' work as a municipal politician and that of as a part-time "Ag Rep," would have made James a known quantity to those in power at Queen's Park.

Also, during his time in municipal politics, James Allan became a member of the Good Roads Association of Ontario, and later became a honourary lifetime member.[5]

However, as 1951 opened, the Ontario General Election loomed and opportunity, in the shape of Leslie Frost and the

Ontario Progressive Conservative party came knocking on James Allan's door.

And James was prepared to answer that prospect.

CHAPTER 6

QUEEN'S PARK BECKONS

IT'S 1951, AND CHARLIE MARTIN, WHO HAD REPRESENTED THE RIDING OF HALDIMAND-Norfolk at Queen's Park since 1944, announced that he was stepping down as MPP. Ontario Premier Leslie Frost, who had taken over leadership of the Ontario Progressive Conservative Party from George Drew in 1949, was heading into his first election as Premier.

Premier Frost wanted the farmer, businessman, dairy owner and long-time municipal politician, James Allan to succeed Charlie Martin as the MPP for Haldimand-Norfolk.

On Thursday, 22 November 1951, Premier Leslie Frost was given the first of the three consecutive majority governments he would form and lead until he stepped down in 1961, continuing the path for what would become a 43-year Tory dynasty that would last until 1985.

Due not only to the popularity of Leslie Frost, but also the reputation that James Allan had, not only in Haldimand County, but in neighbouring Norfolk County as well, the 1951 provincial general election went very well for both James Allan and Leslie Frost.

Premier Davis related to me that he first met James in the office of Thomas Kennedy, the former Premier, and that James came across to the future Premier Davis and everyone else as a very modest and unassuming man who did not seek the spotlight, who always came across as a person who was trustworthy and wise. Premier Davis told the author that James' greatest assets were his leadership qualities and the high level of integrity he carried with him.

James Allan would win handily the election as the MPP for Haldimand-Norfolk by defeating Liberal Elmo Riddle by 2 455 votes. This provincial electoral victory would be the first of six consecutive successes at the provincial ballot box for James Allan until James' defeat by Liberal Gordon Miller in September 1975.

The provincial election of 1951 was also the start of another chapter in the many lives of James Allan. At age 57, which is an age when many of us are looking down the road, over the hill or around the curve of age towards retirement, James Allan looked for his next challenge.

While Premier Davis stated that James started very late as an MPP, James always had a seemingly boundless energy, a vigour that not only appeared to defy age, but that apparently became more unending as he got older.

For the next four years, James Allan was a backbench member of the Ontario Progressive Conservative government. James, when sitting in the Ontario Legislature, would follow the instructions and requests of Premier Frost's various cabinet ministers or the Premier himself.

In an earlier chapter it was mentioned that while James was attending the Ontario Agricultural College in Guelph, he had struck up a lifelong friendship with the future Liberal Premier, Harry Nixon who was from St. George, a sleepy little hamlet north of Brantford.

Harry Nixon had a record for longevity that far eclipsed James' tenure. Harry Nixon was first elected to the Ontario Legislature as the MPP at age 28 in 1919 for the riding of Brant. Harry Nixon held that seat through 12 consecutive provincial elections until his passing at age 70 on 22 October 1961.

Harry Nixon's son, Robert Nixon, succeeded his father in a by-election in 1962 and carried on the tradition of the Nixon family representing the Brant riding for another 29 years, holding the Brant riding for an astounding 71 consecutive years and victorious in 22 successive elections.

Robert Nixon recalled to me meeting James Allan for the first time while his father, Harry Nixon was still the MPP for Brant.

Bob told me that his father always had a very high respect for James and Bob felt that James was an excellent ambassador for Ontario. James had a great sense of humour, was always civilized and intelligent, always a "first-rate" person to deal with in the legislature; James would never attack the person, but the policy.

This behaviour is a far cry from the childish activities, abusive behaviour, churlish and abhorrent conduct of members of the Ontario Legislature that we read and hear of today.

If James Allan was back in Dunnville on an off-day or when the Legislature was not sitting, James would be doing for what he eventually became very well-known for; tirelessly working for his constituents.

In James' day, doing one's constituency work was the norm and what was one was expected to do. Not today when an MP or MPP getting their picture in the paper as much as possible was considered the most important part of their duty. Not getting back to a constituent who was complaining about an unpopular government policy that your government brought in was unheard of.

If you did not do your constituency work properly or at all, you would likely find yourself out of your position after the next election. Unfortunately, the reverse seems to the norm today.

A prime example of how important constituency work was to James Allan, and just how effective James was communicated to this author by the late R. W. Bro. Keith Cosier about two years after this author had joined the Craft at St. Andrew's Masonic Lodge #62 in Caledonia. In 1947 the Opera House, located in Caledonia on the north-east corner of Caithness Street and Argyle Street, was destroyed by a massive fire.[7]

St. Andrew's Lodge, #62 was a tenant of the Opera House, having the Masonic Temple on the third floor of the Opera house. Of course, the total devastation of the Opera House also meant that St. Andrew's Lodge, #62 lost all of their records, Lodge furniture, Officers' collars and jewels.

It took several years for St. Andrew's to re-organize, replace furniture, jewels, etc. while holding their monthly meetings at other Lodge Temples, such as Enniskillen in York, some 5 miles down King's Highway #54.

In late 1951, St. Andrew's had located and made arrangements to purchase a former military barracks from a decommissioned base, likely Malton which was beginning to develop into the Toronto airport hub we now know at Pearson International. That old barracks was destined to be placed where it is presently situated, on Argyle Street North in Caledonia at the CN railroad crossing, in front of the old Anglican Cemetery, across from the Tim Hortons' franchise.

However, to get the old barracks from the base to its desired location could be termed a logistical nightmare.

Along its way, not only would traffic be severely impacted and inconvenienced by the slow pace of the travel, but hydro and other wires that crossed the streets between utility poles would have to be lifted so that the barracks could pass under without damaging the wires. In more than one instance, bridge railings would have to be cut with torches to allow the barracks to pass over the bridge safe and sound. Then those cut railings would have to be welded back together.

Now James had only been elected to the Ontario Legislature on 22 November 1951. However on very short notice, James managed to get provincial and cabinet approval, not only for such a long and considerable move, but also for all the work on bridges and such to allow the barracks to pass securely.

For a brand-new MPP to be able to pull this off for his Masonic brethren a few short months after being elected was quite a coup. This also shows how dedicated James was to his constituents. Whether those constituents were Masonic brethren or not, it did not matter. James Allan did this for everyone in his riding for 24 years.

James Allan became very well-known for, and very adept at, fixing whatever problem, resolve whatever issue or obtain whatever it was that a constituent needed, regardless of the political stripe of the constituent, regardless whether or not that constituent had voted for him. Over the next 24 years, James Allan developed a reputation for not only being a politician who truly worked for all of his constituents, he also became known for not forgetting a face or a name. Premier Davis' one-time Treasurer, Darcy McKeough, told this author that once James met you and got to know your name, James Allan never forgot you.

The author personally experienced this ability of James Allan. In August, 1984 the author was attending an election rally at Simcoe for Brian Mulroney. Now, the author had not seen James Allan since his father's funeral some eleven-and-one-half years earlier in January 1973, and he had only met the author personally once or twice when he was a child on his parents' farm some 15 or 20 years earlier. James Allan was approaching 90 years as well at that time.

Well, needless to say, when James approached the author directly and said, "Hello Allison," the author was both shocked and surprised, and told James so. James just smiled and said he remembered this author from the days when he visited the author's parents' farm.

However the author felt or how it impacted him personally, this type of behaviour and remembering names, etc. was James Allan's trademark and that ability came with both ease and grace.

Harry Bartlett related to me in an interview that James could handle his constituents, and equally well the voters who could be considered a "pain." Harry said that James had a constituency office in the same building that James Allan's Dunnville Dairy was located in.

If an irate constituent came into James' office at the Dunnville Dairy with an issue or other such problem, or one who was known as a chronic pain and complainer, James would greet him near the door, put his arm around their shoulder, listen to the constituent's issue or complaint, all the while quietly and gently guiding that person across his office towards another exit, walking through that second exit door with the person, gently letting them go through, back out onto the street and then closing that second door. This even happened to his good friend, Harry Bartlett, who related to me with a chuckle he did not know it happened until he was on the sidewalk, alone, and the second door to James' office was closed.

Harry Bartlett went on to say that he was once approached by the Ontario Liberal Party in 1967 to run against James, but Harry refused, mostly out of the respect Harry had for James, not only as an MPP but also as a brother Mason.

James Allan was a master of handling people and he had the gift of making you feel you were the only person in the world when you were speaking with him.

James Allan had many unique traits that allowed him to easily deal with people, and he used those traits in the most genuinely unselfish manner possible; helping his fellow man for some two-thirds of his life.

CHAPTER 7
THE PREMIER CALLS TO CABINET

IN 1955, AFTER THE 9 JUNE PROVINCIAL GENERAL ELECTION AND AFTER FOUR YEARS ON THE backbenches of Premier Leslie Frost's Conservative government, the Premier appointed James Allan to his cabinet as the Minister of Highways.

It is noteworthy that not only Premier Frost was a Mason, but the Premier's entire cabinet, save three members, were also Masons. The three who were not Masons were members of the Orange Order and more closely aligned with the Toronto area.

It was obvious what qualities and attributes Premier Frost was looking for in a cabinet minister, and James Allan had what the Premier was seeking.

In those 10 years after the end of WWII, Ontario had been growing rapidly and exponentially in all aspects of its economy.

However, and James had experienced this during his lengthy career in the municipal politics of Haldimand County, the condition of not only the roads of Haldimand County, but virtually all of Ontario's roads needed many and great improvements and additions to its roads system, and Ontario needed it fast.

James was well-known for the capital road improvements that had taken place in Canborough Township, the Town of Dunnville and throughout Haldimand County during his stewardship of James' three-plus decade's time in municipal politics.

As mentioned several times earlier in this book, property owners in Haldimand County, particularly farmers, were expected to grade and maintain the road or roads fronting on their property. This was even stated on your property tax bill and it was only in 1951 that this specific demand was no longer made of rural property owners by Haldimand County.

Now, the administration of President Dwight Eisenhower had recently taken the heady step of putting a 5 cent a gallon tax on gasoline sales. This levy was to pay for a system of limited-access road structures to be built across the United States. We know this scheme now as the Eisenhower Interstate System. Ontario, in order to stay competitive and enjoy continued economic growth, must do the same with its roads, both existing and new.

The Liberal government of Mitchell Hepburn had, during the Great Depression, undertaken some capital road improvements as "make work" projects for unemployed men in the Depression and the improvement of the highways in Haldimand and Norfolk Counties had not been the exception.

The King's Highway system that had begun in 1917 and work on that system had continued into the 1970's, and even beyond.

While what we know now as the Queen Elizabeth Way was built by the Liberal Government of Mitchell Hepburn from 1934 to 1939, the QEW remained, for the most part, the most modern road in Ontario up to, during and after World War II.

The need was great for Ontario to step up and not improve the present road system, but also to design, survey, construct and lay down new provincial highways with new limited access, or what we now know as 400 series, highways. To get it laid down in the swiftest and most cost-efficient manner possible was crucial.

Premier Frost called upon the man who he thought could, and would get that task done.

Over the next three years under the erudite leadership of James Allan, the Ontario Department of Highway was not only able to upgrade many of the existing roads in Ontario, but also constructed some 10 000 miles of new roads.[8]

During James' tenure as Minister of Highways, the King's Highway system was upgraded and increased with capital improvements to outright new King's Highways such as 2A, 7A, 7B up to 133, 134 and 135. Also secondary and tertiary highways like 502, 516 599 and 800 through 813 were planned, began and constructed province-wide under James', and his successors' oversight.

These construction and improvements included connecting, by building the necessary road network in between, the infrastructure that now makes up the modern–day Macdonald-Cartier Freeway or the 401 as we know it today. This flurry of construction also included the start of the first phase of what we know now as Highway 400, which runs from Toronto to Barrie and now onto Parry Sound.

Being Minister of Highways also meant being in charge of the Minister of Highways various 8 000 provincial employees with a then-considerable budget of some $200 000 000.00.[8]

It was also during this time as Minister of Highways that James helped to conceive and bring about what would be his greatest, largest, most visible and longest lasting legacy.

Without up-to-date and modern highways, the economy of Ontario would quickly stagnate and fall behind that of the United States.

So to protect Ontario's economy, someone had to move in the most proactive and cost-efficient manner and get those roads built, and that person was James Allan.

*The M. W. Bro. James Noble Allan, Past Grand Master of the
Grand Lodge of Canada in the Province of Ontario, 1965 - 1967;*

Model of King Solomon's Temple;

Map of Canborough & Canborough Township,
circa 1879, H. R. Page & Co. Atlas;

Farm formerly owned by James & Minerva
Allan, parents of James N. Allan, 2016;

Former Canborough Methodist (United) Church circa 1970;

Site of former Canborough Methodist (United) Church, 2016;

Grand Trunk Railway Station, Dunnville;

Grand Trunk Railway Station & Michigan
Central Railway Tower, Canfield Junction;

Grand Trunk Railway Station, Canfield;

Grand Trunk Railway Station, Caledonia;

The Honourable Harry Nixon, premier of Ontario, 1943 & OAC classmate of James N. Allan;

James N. Allan graduation photo, 1914;

OLD DUNNVILLE
CREAMERY

Dunnville Dairy

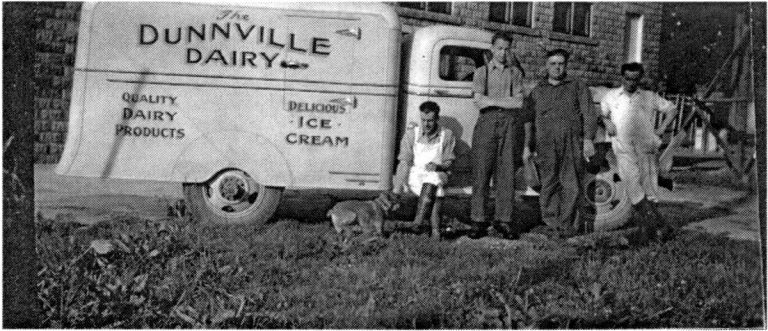

Former Dunnville Dairy, Dunnville Creamery, vehicles &
employees (unknown), circa 1930 - 1940, photographs courtesy of,
and with thanks to the Dunnville District Heritage Association;

Demolition of the former Dunnville Dairy building,
circa 1994, photographs courtesy of, and with thanks
to the Dunnville District Heritage Association

Dunnville Dairy bottle, 2016, photographs courtesy of, and with thanks to the Dunnville District Heritage Association

Former Dunnville Dairy building, 2016;

Grace United Church, Dunnville, circa 1960;

The Honourable Leslie Frost, Premier of Ontario, 1949 – 1961;

Construction of Burlington Bay Skyway, circa 1955;

Construction of Burlington Bay Skyway, circa 1956;

On December 13, 1957, the final 57 foot top steel cord was put into place in the 210 foot high Centre Span over the Burlington Ship Canal.

Construction of Burlington Bay Skyway, circa 1957;

Construction of Burlington Bay Skyway, circa 1958;

Burlington Bay Skyway toll booth;

Burlington Bay Skyway toll booth & toll collector;

Burlington Bay Skyway toll booth & toll collector;

Burlington Bay Skyway token;

Burlington Bay Skyway token;

Burlington Bay Skyway package of tokens;

Burlington Bay Skyway & Burlington Ship
Canal Lift Bridge, circa 1970;

Amity Masonic Lodge, #32, A.F. & A.M., Dunnville, circa 1970;

The Honourable John Robarts, Premier of Ontario 1961 – 1971;

*The Honourable William Davis, Premier
of Ontario 1971 – 1984;*

Allan Family headstone, cemetery markers of James N. Allan
& Lilian Harvie Allan and Harvie Allan & Phyllis Allan;

CHAPTER 8
THE SKYWAY

AS STATED IN AN EARLIER CHAPTER, THE TIME AFTER WORLD WAR II, FROM 1945 TO 1960 was a decade-and-a-half of huge and rapid economic growth for Ontario, in agriculture, in commerce, in industry and in urban expansion.

However at that time the two main railroads, the Canadian National Railway, or CNR and the Canadian Pacific Railway, or CPR were beginning to scale back their operations in Ontario and Eastern Canada. The railroads were starting to concentrate the majority of their operations in Western Canada in shipping and transporting western commodities where profits were larger.

As well, both the CNR and the CPR had long been suspected of grievously over-charging their customers, especially the rural clientele, for decades, which resulted in more trucks and other delivery vehicles on Ontario's roads. This was also a compelling force in Ontario, which James Allan understood.

By the end of the 1950's, neither the CNR nor CPR was running an inter-urban railway service in Ontario any longer. Instead, both the CNR and CPR were choosing to concentrate on freight operations in Ontario for the time being.

This reduction in service meant large industrial operations, such as the new automobile assembly plant that the Ford Motor Company had built in Oakville had to bring in more and more parts and supplies by relying upon tractor-trailers coming into the Ford plant in Oakville on the QEW.

Also, when James had to travel between his home in Dunnville and Queen's Park, at first if desired, James could have taken the train from Dunnville to Toronto, via Caledonia and Hamilton. However, interurban steam train service in Ontario and this author believes all of Canada, ended on 26 October 1957. So if James wanted to get to Toronto, or get home, he had to drive from Dunnville via the various King's Highways and the QEW, then into downtown Toronto.

However, at the Burlington Ship Canal which was the entrance and exit between Hamilton Harbour and Lake Ontario, the QEW chicaned from four lanes down to two lanes where the QEW crossed the canal via the Burlington Lift Bridge.

Now, it was congested enough with the narrowing from four lanes to two lanes of the QEW at the canal. If a ship was approaching the Burlington lift bridge to enter or exit the harbour, the lift bridge would have to be raised to allow that ship pass under the lift bridge. If that lift bridge was up, you could count a very, very long wait for that ship to pass and the bridge to come down.

This author recalls his parents telling him about the times that they were caught in the traffic back-up at the lift bridge on their trips to and from Toronto. The line-up of cars waiting for the bridge to be lowered could be as long as three miles in either direction. Even when the bridge went down, it would be just as long, even possibly a longer time for the line-ups of cars to dissipate and traffic to return to normal.

James, like any other driver, would have likely been so tired and fed up with the wait at the lift bridge; he would have not been above musing about a bridge that would be high enough to allow the ships to pass without disrupting the traffic on the QEW. Many, many other drivers on the QEW at that time in history felt the same way.

It needed to be built quickly. While the idea of a high-level bridge over the Burlington Ship Canal was seen as visionary by some people, just as many of the populace equally viewed the idea of a high-level bridge as folly.

Although that idea of a high level bridge to span the ship canal had been around since before the completion of the QEW in 1939, it was not until a ship, the W. E. Fitzgerald, struck and severely damaged the lift bridge over the ship canal in 1953 that a high-level bridge over the Burlington ship canal became a very serious thought.[9] This accident and subsequent repairs caused massive traffic delays and the cries for the province to do something, not just from the drivers of automobiles but also the truck drivers and trucking companies, to alleviate the traffic bottleneck at the ship canal were growing louder, longer and larger.

The W. E. Fitzgerald accident finally propelled the Ministry of Highways into action, and their engineers had drawn up preliminary plans and costs, which were then presented to the

Premier and cabinet with James Allan, who had become the driving force behind the Skyway project several years before.

Soon final plans were drawn up and tenders given out for the bridge construction. The shovels and equipment went into the ground and construction got under way sometime in 1954 or 1955 with completion slated for fall 1958. The Burlington Bay Skyway opened to traffic on 30 October 1958.[9]

The construction of this high-level bridge was expected to possibly cost in excess of $15 000 000.00, and in fact eventually did cost $19 000 000.00.[8]

The bridge which was named the Burlington Bay Skyway, much to the consternation of Hamilton City Council who wanted a name for the bridge to reflect more of a Hamilton connection.

For the first 14 years of the operation of the Burlington Bay Skyway it was a toll bridge. At the end of October 1972, the toll booths went down and no longer would a driver have to stop and dig into their pockets for nickels and dimes before crossing the bridge.

A popular myth was the reason for the cessation of the collection of tolls was the traffic back-ups caused by cars and trucks stopping to pay the bridge tolls. However, the author recall his mother telling him that the province stopped taking tolls at the end of October 1972 was because the provincial legislation that created the Burlington Bay Skyway stated that a toll would be collected from each vehicle crossing the Skyway until the bridge was fully paid for. And at the end of October 1972 the bridge was paid for. So the toll booths came down shortly thereafter.

This policy of collecting tolls until the bridge way paid for continued with the later construction of the Garden City Skyway over the Welland Canal at St. Catharines.

The author recollects when he and his mother were preparing to move to Caledonia after she sold the family farm in June 1973 after the author's father passed away in January 1973. The author came across three or four of those little bronze tokens you would be able to purchase, four for 10 cents, for the tolls on the Burlington Bay Skyway. The author asked his mother what to do with them and he was told they were useless as the Skyway was no longer a toll bridge. So he threw the tokens out. The author often wonders now what those little bronze tokens would fetch today from a collector of such memorabilia.

As we know, Ontario, and especially the GTA, has enjoyed continued growth through the 1960's and 1970's and soon the Skyway was over-crowded and congested throughout most of the day, just not at rush hour.

So plans were drawn up for the "twinning" of the Skyway. In 1985 the second span of the Skyway was opened, making eight lanes of traffic on the QEW over the Burlington Ship Canal.

To those of us who have used the Skyway many times over the past 30 years, it seems that even eight lanes are still not enough at certain periods.

On James Allan's 90th birthday in 1984 it was announced that, to mark his vision, his drive, his leadership and his involvement in the construction of the original span of the Skyway, was renamed "The Burlington Bay James N. Allan Skyway." This granted recognition to James Allan's significant contribution to the planning and construction of the Skyway, as well as his equally noteworthy involvement in working to shape the Ontario we know today.

Bob Nixon related to this author that there was a great deal of debate and criticism at the time of including James' name on the Skyway, but the majority of that criticism came from the MPP's and others who were too young, or not even born, to remember the hard work, contributions and legacy of James Allan.

However, placing the name of James N. Allan on the Burlington Bay Skyway was still a fitting gift for, and tribute to one of Ontario's great leaders, visionaries and statesmen.

Now you have the answer for that trivia question that surfaces on Hamilton radio stations periodically, "Who is the Burlington Bay Skyway named after?"

CHAPTER 9

BRINGING "FROSTBITE" TO ONTARIO

IT WAS 1958, AND PREMIER LESLIE FROST HAD BEEN LEADING THE ONTARIO PROGRESSIVE Conservative Party and the Province of Ontario for nine years. And the Premier decided it was time to divest himself of some of the cabinet duties Frost had taken responsibility for since becoming leader.

As well, as with any government, whether in the past or of the current day, the Government of Ontario was always looking for new and more revenue streams to help pay for its various programs and capital projects.

So Leslie Frost turned to one of his most capable and trusted lieutenants, James Allan. Leslie Frost moved James from Minister of Highways in the spring of 1958 to be Minister of Transportation.

However, in December 1958, Premier Frost promoted James to the portfolio of the Minister, Department of Economics, or what was later called the Treasurer and today is known as the Minister of Finance.

It is commonly acknowledged that whoever holds the post of Minister, Department of Economics, Treasurer, Minister of Finance or whatever you wish to call the position, is considered to the Premier's "right-hand man," or simply put, the second-most powerful person in the Government of Ontario, next to the Premier.

Shortly after becoming the Minister, Department of Economics, the Premier charged James with developing, introducing and selling a political time-bomb to the electorate of Ontario, a provincial sales tax.

It has been all through history, ancient or modern, when governments introduce a new tax, people generally are not happy. Even when the introduction takes place in good economic times, people are generally not too thrilled. But usually a much, much worse reception is given out if the new tax is levied in bad economic times. One only has to look back to the federal election of 1993 when Canadians took out their frustration with the hated Goods & Services Tax levied by Prime Minister Brian Mulroney in 1991 in the most vicious manner, reducing the federal Progressive Conservative party to just two seats in Parliament.

In 1959, the economy in Ontario was enjoying a reasonably prosperous economic time. However, on 20 February 1959, on what later became was known as "Black Friday," the economy in the GTA, more specifically the Peel County, Brampton, Bramalea, Mississauga regions, suffered a hugely brutal blow. This was the day when the Diefenbaker government announced it was cancelling the Avro Arrow project. The Avro Arrow jet fighter and interceptor was at that time currently under development and construction at the A. V. Roe plant in Malton, ON, next to the Malton (now Pearson International) Airport.

With the euphemistic "stroke of the pen," the Diefenbaker Conservative government put 14 528 A. V. Roe employees out of work. Most of these people who lived locally, were working on the Arrow project, and were suddenly unemployed. Traditionally people, when suddenly hit with a calamity of this nature, will take it out on the nearest government at the next earliest time, which would usually be at the next election, whether it be a federal or a provincial election.

Premier Davis imparted to me that, at the time of "Black Friday," C. D. Howe, who had been a key member of Prime Minister Mackenzie King's and Louis St. Laurent's cabinet for many years and who had held many vital cabinet positions, such as Minister of Finance and Minister of Munitions and Supply, for King before, during and after WWII, strongly believed that the United States military would be the major purchaser of the Arrow. We know now that was not the case. However, hindsight is always 20/20. Or as the author's grandfather used to say, "If hindsight were foresight, we'd need no sight at all."

Premier Leslie Frost was scheduled to call a provincial general election in the spring of 1959. The cancellation of the Avro Arrow project was an incredibly major blow to the local, and provincial, economy and posed a huge threat to the Frost regime. So with that cancellation of the Avro Arrow program, with nearly 15 000 people suddenly out of work as a result, this had major implications for Frost with that spring election in the offing.

When former Premier William Davis was interviewed for this book, he related to this author his first-hand experience with the cancellation of the Arrow and its effect on Ontario, specifically Leslie Frost.

The Premier said that he was in Premier Frost's office at Queen's Park a meeting on that fateful day, as Frost had invited Premier Davis to run in the provincial riding of Peel to replace the retiring former Progressive Conservative Premier, Thomas Kennedy in the election expected in the spring of 1959.

The future Premier was having a conversation with Premier Frost when the news of the Arrow cancellation reached Premier Frost. Needless to say, Premier Frost was very shocked at the news as he had not expected anything like this.

Premier Davis related to this author that Premier Frost immediately turned to his telephone and dialed the direct number for Prime Minister John Diefenbaker's office in Ottawa.

The Premier remarked to me that Premier Frost had an incredibly animated conversation with the Prime Minister and Premier Davis remarked that, "Mr. Frost used words I had never heard him use before!"

However, despite the terrible economic shock caused by the federal government's abandonment of the Arrow project and nearly 15 000 workers, and with Leslie Frost being the very masterful politician he was, Premier Frost received his third consecutive majority government later that spring.

Nevertheless, both the Premier and James knew how volatile the electorate, whether it was for a federal, provincial or municipal issue, can be. Bringing in a new tax, any type of tax, had to be handled in just the right manner or it could literally explode in your face.

The drafting, creation and introduction, along with the daunting task of convincing Ontarians of the need for the revenue that the new sales tax would bring, how it would help finance the many projects planned for Ontario that would help shape its future, had been squarely placed into the lap of James Allan.

Her Majesty's Loyal Opposition at the time, the Liberal Party of Ontario under John Winterweyer, along with the newspapers of the day, dubbed the government's proposed sales tax as "Frostbite," a barb directly aimed at Premier Frost.

However at that time, while Premier Frost's Tories enjoyed a plurality of 22 seats from the 1959 election, that being a majority in the Legislature, there was never any doubt as to the successful passage of that legislation.

The real task was selling Ontarians on "Frostbite," and the need for the government of the revenue that this tax would bring.

James was also entrusted with the task of ensuring that the electorate of Ontario would not take it out on the Frost government in the next election, expected in 1963.

The initial rate for the Ontario Retail Sales Tax would be three per cent on a majority of the goods and services that Ontarians used. James' people skills, his gift of oratory and the fact that many people, even those who had only just met him, trusted him and what he said, he was able to sell "Frostbite" to Ontarians and the government's need for that revenue.

How effective was James Allan in selling Ontarians on the Ontario Retail Sales Tax?

In the election of 1959, Leslie Frost's majority of seats were reduced from 83 seats to 71 seats in the Legislature.

In the election of 1963, under Premier Frost's successor, Premier John Robarts, the Tories increased their number of seats from 71 seats to 77 seats. It was obvious that James Allan had done the job of selling "Frostbite" extremely well.

The efforts, talents and abilities of James Allan did not go unnoticed in the world outside of politics and Queen's Park. In 1961, McMaster University in Hamilton conferred upon James Allan an Honourary Doctorate of Laws or "Honoris Causa."

So now, it was "Dr. James Allan," but to the many that knew him, in Haldimand-Norfolk, in business, in politics, at Queen's Park, in cabinet, all over Ontario, even in Masonic Lodges, it was just, still was and always would be just plain "Jim."

The face of the new Ontario Retail Sales Tax, or "Frostbite" was not Leslie Frost, and it was not John Robarts, it was James Allan, a rural Ontario farmer turned successful business-man and municipal politician who had worked his way up to become one of the most important politicians in Ontario. He was also one of the most vital players in the machinery of the Government of Ontario.

However, this was not the beginning of the end for James Allan, but more possibilities, successes and accolades were building on the horizon as well as a disappointment.

CHAPTER 10

A QUIET LEADER...PERHAPS A PREMIER IN WAITING?

IT IS NOW 1961; LESLIE FROST HAS BEEN LEADER OF THE PROGRESSIVE CONSERVATIVE Party and Premier of Ontario for 12 years and has won a majority of seats in three consecutive provincial elections, in 1951, 1955 and 1959. This is considered a highly prized and coveted benchmark for any premier and for a dynasty, both provincially and federally. The Premier decides it is time to step down, so Leslie Frost announces his retirement and calls on the Ontario Progressive Conservative Party to have a leadership convention to choose a new leader and Premier.

Soon after Frost's retirement was announced, there was a host of veteran Progressive Conservative MPP's who announced they were running to replace Leslie Frost. Party stalwarts such as Kelso Roberts, John Robarts, Robert Macaulay, A.W. Downer, Matthew Dymond, and George Wardrope were all interested.

However, there was one name that was missing from that horde of MPP's. A missing name that had become a household name all over Ontario the past six years, that of James Allan.

While James Allan was some 10 months older than Leslie Frost, who was stepping down at age 66, many viewed James Allan as the most able successor to Leslie Frost. James was viewed as such for his gifted handling of both of the Highway and Transportation portfolios along with the construction of the Burlington Bay Skyway, not to mention of his exceptionally skillful management of the Treasurer's portfolio and of the implementation of "Frostbite" or the first Ontario Retail Sales Tax.

While many of the MPP's in the Progressive Conservative caucus encouraged James to run from the beginning of the race for the leadership because of both his record and his popularity within Ontario, James vacillated about running. There were likely very good reasons that prevented James from entering the race to replace Frost right at the beginning of the leadership contest. However, only James knew those reasons.

When Premier Davis, who was one of James' closest cabinet and caucus colleagues for some 15 years, was interviewed for this manuscript he advised this author that he finally convinced James to run for the leadership, even though Premier Davis was committed to another contender. Premier Davis went on to state that James, who was a commanding presence at the cabinet table, with all of his great attributes and personal popularity; would have made a great premier.

But while James Allan did eventually "throw his hat" into the ring to replace Leslie Frost, unfortunately, James' entry came too late. Many of the sitting Progressive Conservative MPP's, including those who had initially encouraged James to run, had committed themselves to other leadership candidates after it seemed to them that James Allan was not going to run to replace Frost.

It would have been political suicide for any MPP to pull support for one leadership candidate for another who enters the race at a later date.

However, James Allan was a masterful politician, skillful at working a crowd or simply speaking with one or two people.

Darcy McKeough, who later went on to represent the riding of Kent West and later Chatham Kent from 1963 to 1978, recalled meeting James Allan for the first time at the 1961 leadership convention. Darcy went on to advise this author that he was "awestruck" by James, his warmth and personality. Darcy told me that he learned a great deal from James, and that James was always available for questions, for advice and he was very impressed at James' capacity for remembering faces and names.

Darcy went to tell this author that James strongly encouraged him to run for the Progressive Conservative leadership in 1971. Darcy finished third behind the victor, Bill Davis and endorsed Bill Davis on his exit from the race, and the runner-up, Allan Lawrence. After the leadership race, Premier Davis appointed Darcy to cabinet as Treasurer of Ontario.

Darcy advised me that, after James' electoral defeat in 1975, he visited James several time at James' home in Dunnville.

Darcy says he remembers James' assets the most, his memory, his penchant for remembering faces and names, his towering integrity and his devotion to Ontario.

When I interviewed Robert Nixon, the former leader of the Liberal Party of Ontario, he recalled to me that his father, former Premier Harry Nixon, had passed away on 22 October

1961, just three days before the Progressive Conservative delegates would be voting for a new leader and Premier.

Robert Nixon related to me that his father's funeral was held on the morning of the leadership convention's voting day. The outgoing Premier, Leslie Frost was the only member of the Progressive Conservative caucus to attend and pay his respects. The leadership convention had pushed back the time for the voting to start because of Harry Nixon's funeral.

Bob advised that he later received many sympathies on the passing of his father and many apologies from members of the Progressive Conservative cabinet, caucus and party for being unable to attend.

The day for the leadership vote was to be held in the University of Toronto's Varsity Arena on Wednesday, 25 October 1961. At that time, each riding would be eligible to send a certain number of delegates to the convention and each delegate would have a vote on each ballot for the leadership. As well, all sitting MPP's and the defeated candidates from the ridings the Tories did not win in the previous election along with the Progressive Conservative party executives would have a vote as well.

There were a total of 1 710 delegates eligible to vote at the Progressive Conservative leadership convention in 1961, made up of MPP's, non-victorious candidates in the previous election and party executives, so in order for whatever candidate to win the leadership, and the position of Premier, need 50 per cent, plus one vote, was needed to win. At this convention, a minimum of 856 votes would be required to win the Progressive Conservative party leadership and the Premier's chair.

With seven candidates vying for Leslie's Frost's job, there could conceivably be six ballots to decide who would replace Leslie Frost in the position of leader and Premier.

As was the custom with leadership races, if there was no clear winner on a ballot, whatever candidate who had placed last on that ballot count was required to drop off prior to the next ballot. That candidate's supporters sometimes would be directed to another candidate by way of an endorsement by that last-place candidate. Or they would be released by the defeated candidate to be allowed to vote for whomever they wished.

The first ballot was close; there were only 20 votes between first-place candidate Kelso Roberts and fourth-place aspirant James Allan.

However, while the second, third and fourth ballots did not provide a clear winner, the two leading candidates, Kelso Roberts and John Robarts both slowly increased the number of votes they received with each passing ballot. However, James Allan's support remained fixed between 324 and 344 votes over those first four ballots. When James finished last on the fourth ballot with 336 votes, he was forced to drop out of the 1961 leadership race.

However, the voting to replace Leslie Frost took another two ballots until John Robarts was declared the winner over Kelso Roberts on the sixth ballot.

As a reflection on how highly James Allan's abilities were valued, not just by John Robarts, but by the Ontario Progressive Conservative party and the caucus, the new Premier, John Robarts, left James in his portfolio as Treasurer. What this reflection meant is that while it was the common practice of whoever had finished second to the new leader in the leadership contest, the Premier would have usually appointed that second-place finisher to the Treasurer's portfolio as the new Premier's "right-hand man." Leaving James Allan in the Treasurer's portfolio was testament to his abilities and how highly he was regarded by the new Premier and the Progressive Conservative caucus.

To just look ahead at history, the next Progressive Conservative leadership contest would not be held until 1971, some 10 years later and James Allan would be almost 77 years old, far too old to be reasonably considered for the job of leader and Premier. So the Progressive Conservative leadership race of 1961 was the first, last and only chance James Allan would have had to become leader and Premier.

This author has been very fortunate to have been able to speak to several of the few people still living that knew James Allan well, and all say that James Allan's belated entry and delayed start into the 1961 Progressive Conservative leadership race cost him too many potential delegates and crucial votes. These issues and lost votes proved to be an obstacle that even that great politician James Allan could not overcome, no matter how skillful and how popular a politician James was.

In short, the leadership aspirations and campaign of James Allan in the 1961 Progressive Conservative leadership contest was doomed from the start. For what could be construed as the only malfunction in a long and storied 60 year political career, James' sharp political instincts failed him this one time.

What would the landscape of Ontario have looked like if James had been elected leader of the Ontario Progressive Conservative party and Premier in 1961 instead of John Robarts? What would the possible Premiership have meant to James Allan and his Masonic ambitions? What would have a James Allan victory meant to caucus colleagues such as William Davis and others 10 years down the road?

However, as interesting as these questions may be, we can never answer them, nor will these questions ever be answered. Simply, we will never know what Ontario would have been like under the leadership of Premier James Noble Allan because this did not happen.

However, as it will be shown in later chapters of this book, James' defeat in the 1961 leadership race was very far from being the end of James' career at Queen's Park.

.

CHAPTER 11

A BUSY GRAND MASTER

OVER ALL OF THE YEARS THAT JAMES ALLAN HAD BEEN INVOLVED IN THE DUNNVILLE DAIRY, his municipal political career and then his occupation at Queen's Park, James managed another parallel calling. That career was being an ardent and practising Mason.

Ever since James Allan has begun his Masonic career at Amity Masonic Lodge #32 in Dunnville in 1918, James has worked his way up the ladder, not just at Amity Lodge #32, but through the Niagara District "A" and through Grand Lodge of Canada in the Province of Ontario.

For every year from 1931 to 1988, for 57 years, James Allan attended the Annual Communication of the Grand Lodge of Canada in the Province of Ontario as a member of Amity Lodge #32 in Dunnville, ON.[13] In some years, the Annual Communication was held in Hamilton, which was easily reached from Dunnville. However, in later years, the Annual

Communication had been, and continues to be held in Toronto and the Annual Communication is headquartered downtown at the Royal York Hotel.

While today, a journey into Toronto is not that difficult as it is frustrating, with a fairly modern highway system you can get into downtown Toronto with reasonable ease.

However, from the 1930's through to the late 1950's it proved otherwise. The highways into Toronto were not that good and there was no Gardiner Expressway until the early 1960's. You could take the train from Dunnville, but that meant changing trains at Caledonia and again at Hamilton.

But James persevered each year, travelling to the Annual Communication every year since being elected to Grand Lodge as the District Deputy Grand Master for Niagara District "A" in 1931 until 1988 when age and infirmity severely restricted his travel.

In 1947,[10] R. W. Bro. James Allan was appointed by the Grand Master of the day, our M. W. Bro. C. S. Hamilton, and again in 1949,[10] R. W. Bro. James Allan by our M. W. Bro. J. P. Maher to serve on the Board of General Purposes of Grand Lodge of Canada in the Province of Ontario. It was obvious that these two Grand Masters knew where to look for talent to assist the Board of General Purposes.

Then in July 1951, some four months before James was elected to the Provincial Legislature at Queen's Park for the first time, James was elected to the Board of General Purposes of Grand Lodge of Canada in the Province of Ontario.[12]

The Board of General Purposes is like a "board of directors" for Grand Lodge. All committee work, planning, operating Grand Lodge, overseeing the entire member Lodges in Ontario, etc. was done by the Board of General Purposes, usually in conjunction with each Masonic district's District Deputy Grand Master.

Over the next 12 years, after being elected to the Legislature as the MPP for Haldimand-Norfolk in 1951, James was promoted to cabinet in 1955 as the Minister of Highways, then moved to be the Minister of Transportation in the summer of 1958. Five months later, he was promoted to what we now know as the Treasurer, the second-most powerful person in the Government of Ontario. Then next, mounting an unsuccessful bid to be the leader of the Ontario Progressive Conservative Party leader and Premier of Ontario, James Allan was also, at the same time, an incredibly active Mason and member of the Board of General Purposes of Grand Lodge of Canada in the Province of Ontario.

At the time of James' election to Board of General Purposes of Grand Lodge of Canada in the Province of Ontario and election to the Legislature in 1951, he was 58. As stated in an earlier chapter, a person in their late 50's may be starting to look ahead to at time when they can retire. Yet here is James Allan, ramping up the activity in his life in a most significant manner.

A major part of a member's duties, whether the appointment was that of being an elected member, an appointed member or a honourary member to the Board of General Purposes was Masonic committee work. Beyond a member's attendance at the various Grand Masters' Receptions held throughout the province over the Grand Master's two-year term, this was sometimes known, "tongue-in-cheek," as "the rubber chicken circuit."

From 1947, when James was first appointed a member of the Board of General Purposes (BGP), through 1951 when he was first elected to the Board of General Purposes, and in 1963 and 1965 when James was elected to the post of Deputy

Grand Master, then Grand Master and then James'"post" Grand Master time through to his passing to the Grand Lodge Above in 1992, he continued to sit on many Grand Lodge committees.

The author's search of the Annual Proceedings of the Grand Lodge of Canada in the Province of Ontario from 1919 through to 1992 shows the activity and commitment of the Past Grand Master, our M. W. Bro. James N. Allan [13]:

- ✦ Advisory Board: 1984–1987
- ✦ Audit & Finance: 1949-1952, 1963-1964, 1968-1990
- ✦ Benevolence: 1953-1964, 1961-1963 (Chair 60-62)
- ✦ Constitution & Jurisprudence: 1963-1964, 1967, 1968-1991
- ✦ Discipline: 1989-1990
- ✦ Fraternal Correspondence: 1972-1981
- ✦ Fraternal Relations: 1963-1964, 1969-1981
- ✦ Grievances & Appeals: 1947-1953, 1955, 1969-1987
- ✦ Lodge Re-assessment: 1971-1985
- ✦ Masonic Education: 1951-1958, 1963
- ✦ Masonic Foundation:1962-1963, 1976, 1979-1981
- ✦ Masonic Holdings: 1980-1991
- ✦ Masonic Task Force: 1983
- ✦ President, BGP: 1963-1964
- ✦ Regalia: 1980
- ✦ Warrants: 1954-1957, 1959, 1963 (Chair, 1956-1957, 1959)

To be anecdotal; if you can imagine, it is 1961, your day job is being responsible for the finances of Ontario, the largest province in Canada along with being Haldimand-Norfolk's representative at Queen's Park. Your "night" job, which embodies your passion, nurtures you and gives you the direction and morals for the lifestyle you are expected to lead as a member of the largest fraternity in the world that dates its origins to the building of King Solomon's Temple at Jerusalem, anticipates you assisting in the operation and overseeing of the largest fraternal organization in world.

At the same time, in 1961, you decide to run for the leadership of the political party you are member of and represent your home riding for and if successful in the Ontario Progressive Conservative Party's leadership race, you will then be the Premier of the largest province in Canada.

The workload that James Allan would have likely had at that time is simply bewildering and it perplexes and amazes the mind of this author and many others today. If any of us had the workload of James Allan had in the early and mid 1960's, one honestly thinks that none of us in this day and age could handle such an intense responsibility.

Then to increase that workload, in 1963 James ran for, and was elected to, the position of Deputy Grand Master. This also increased James' workload exponentially for the next two years. However, this rise in James' labours was only a harbinger of what more was to come.

James Allan, in 1965, took the next step and was elected the Grand Master of the Grand Lodge of Canada in the Province of Ontario

In 1966, when James Allan was STILL the Treasurer of Ontario in the Robarts' government and when James was halfway through his two-year term as Grand Master of the Grand Lodge of Canada in the Province of Ontario, James stepped down as Treasurer of Ontario.

When Premier William Davis was interviewed, he recalled that particular instance as somewhat humourous, and it was stated Premier Davis told James Allan that James was going into "semi-retirement."

While it was true that while James was relinquishing the Treasurer portfolio, he was staying on as a member of the Robarts' cabinet as a member "without portfolio."

At the age of 72, James Allan, who also jokingly referred to himself as "semi-retired," but also was still the sitting MPP for Haldimand-Norfolk, serving on various legislative committees as part of being an MPP, James was, as well, performing as an important part of the provincial cabinet of Premier John Robarts as a minister "without portfolio." Meanwhile, he was expected to attend weekly cabinet meetings, offer his opinion, advice, etc. on various provincial matters and issues of importance. He also continued his constituency work in his home riding, with appearances on behalf of the government and the Premier.

That amount of work sounds like one of a first cousin of this author who, at age 80, said that "semi-retirement" meant he did not work Sundays any more.

And James also had a rigorous and arduous schedule as Grand Master for his two-year term, expected to not only attend the various Grand Master receptions throughout the 35 districts in Ontario at that time, but there would be travel to other Masonic jurisdictions, not just in Canada, but also to the many of the different Grand Lodge sessions, conferences and meetings in the 50 Masonic jurisdictions in the United States as well. The Grand Master even worked in a visit to Masonic jurisdictions in England. He also accepted the expected work in James' own Masonic sphere of the Grand Lodge of Canada in the Province of Ontario with committee meetings, engagements with the Board of General Purposes and dealing with his own 35 District Deputy Grand Masters for each of his two years. This meant not only reading all of the various reports of District Deputy Grand Masters and District Secretaries on their annual visits and the state of their district's finances and other issues, but also looking over copies of the Lodge summons from each Masonic Lodge in Ontario.[14]

In the Masonic year of 1965 – 1966, as Grand Master James Allan, in addition to receptions throughout Ontario, Grand Lodge work and other Masonic duties, visited the Grand Lodges of Illinois, Ohio, Maryland, Pennsylvania, Massachusetts, Minnesota, Main, New York, Michigan, Manitoba, Quebec, Wisconsin and Nova Scotia.

In the Masonic year of 1966 – 1967, as Grand Master James Allan attended the Grand Masters' and Grand Secretary's Conference in Washington, the Canadian Conferences of Grand & District Grand Lodges visited the Grand Lodges of Illinois, Ohio, Pennsylvania, New York, New Brunswick, Indiana, Michigan, Quebec, Wisconsin and the Grand Lodge of England as well as the Supreme Council of Ancient & Accepted Scottish Rite of Freemasonry.

Over the course of James Allan's two-year term as Grand Master there would be various Lodge consecrations, centennial celebrations, institutions, constituted, dedicated and other Masonic functions. Such occasions as funerals, Masonic Memorial Services and presentation of 50 or 60 years pins, to name a few.

There would be the usual felicitations, appreciations, and of course the "not so pleasant" aspects of dealing with disciplinary actions against members who had violated their Masonic obligations.

However, what our M. W. Bro. James Allan described as one of the largest highlights of his two-year term as Grand Master was the dedication of the new Lodge building for James Allan's mother Lodge, Amity Lodge, #32 in Dunnville. This was an incredible source of pride and satisfaction for the Grand Master.

Another highlight James Allan described was attending the Annual Meeting of the Supreme Council of Ancient & Accepted Scottish Rite of Freemasonry in Niagara Falls and being the keynote speaker at the luncheon.

The work involved in being a Grand Master for two years, with the workload involved, would be full-time position for a person who is already retired from their regular and personal vocation.

However, here is James Allan, who was still a sitting MPP and a cabinet minister, first Treasurer, then a minister without portfolio, all of which is more than a full-time employment on its own, and he manages to manage, quite successfully, the significant duties and responsibilities of both of these positions. This speaks to the incredible drive, aptitude, abilities and capacities of James Allan.

In each of James' years, 1965 – 1966 and 1966 – 1967, the Grand Master's District Deputy Grand Masters reported that the Lodges in their various Districts to be in fine shape, both financially and in regards to membership.

James Allan was also being the spiritual and titular leader of some 132 000 Masons throughout Ontario at that time.

As stated earlier, James Allan was a simple, humble man who went about his work, both in Masonry and in his everyday life, to make better the lives of his fellow man.

In the Grand Lodge Proceedings of 1966, James' efforts to reach out to Masons in Ontario were duly noted;[15]

> *"The many years that our Grand Master has devoted to the cause of public service and the many offices of leadership which he has filled have enabled M.W. Bro. J. N. Allan to bring the office of Grand Master just a little closer to the average member. His success had made it possible for him to present his explanation of Masonic ideals in a very intimate way to his Brethren. It can be truly said that M.W. Bro. Allan is maintaining the wonderful level of quality in leadership which has been given to this Grand Lodge by his illustrious predecessors in office."*

One of the Grand Master's visits was to Shuniah Lodge, No. 287 in Port Arthur (now a part of Thunder Bay) to honour Bro. John A. Walker on 77 years of membership in Shuniah Lodge.[16] Even the Grand Master was not a Mason for that long. When the Grand Master passed away in May, 1992, he was in his 74th year of membership in the Craft.

One also has to realize that the last six months of James Allan's term of Grand Master also would have coincided with the six-month run-up to Canada's Centennial celebration and the then-Dominion Day, now Canada Day festivities. These six months, as those of us who are old enough would remember, would have been filled with many different Centennial celebrations within our communities or festivities that were municipally, provincially or federally sponsored.

The Grand Master also led the Grand Lodge of Canada in the Province of Ontario in assisting in the celebration of the

250th anniversary of the establishment of modern Freemasonry in England in 1717.

As well, during M. W. Bro. James Allan's tenure as Deputy Grand Master, the Masonic Foundation of Ontario, a Masonic charity, was founded. The Foundation quickly became one of James Allan's passions and he served on the Grand Lodge committee that oversees the Foundation for several years

It is fitting that such leadership, fellowship and camaraderie that would emanate from such a person as our M. W. Bro. James N. Allan that he was chosen to lead Masonry during such auspicious events as a national centennial and an international fraternal sestercentennial anniversaries.

In Masonry, in the jurisdiction of the Grand Lodge of Canada in the Province of Ontario, the legacy of our M. W. Bro. James N. Allan still lives on in the simplest manner.

Another of our esteemed Past Grand Masters, our M. W. Bro. Gary L. Atkinson (2005 – 2007) was given, and still proudly wears and displays the same regalia of our late brother, our M. W. Bro. James N. Allan, wore for his two-year term as Grand Master.

It is a fitting salute that the legacy and remembrance M. W. Bro. James N. Allan lives on in the Craft, even in this most simple, but honourable, method.

One of James Allan's earliest decisions as Grand Master can still be seen at every Grand Master's Reception, no matter what district you may be in.

Harry Bartlett, who was James Allan's Grand Director of Ceremonies in 1966 - 1967, related to me that at all of the previous Grand Master's Receptions, the members of the Board of General Purposes would usually sequester themselves at tables with their wives.

Harry shared with me that James felt that this behaviour gave the potential impression that the members of the Board of General Purposes were a private club or a "coffee clutch."

James decreed that, starting at the next Grand Master's Reception, the members of the Board of General Purposes and their wives would be spread out all through the banquet seating, one member and his spouse at each table. This would increase the meetings and connections between the various members of the Board of General Purposes and other members of the Masonic fraternity.

That is still done today at all the Grand Master's Receptions.

All this legislative, cabinet, committee and constituency work AND the massive schedule of Masonic labours such as the Board of General Purposes meetings, committee work, banquets and other appearances or receptions for a man who turned 71 four months after being the elected Grand Master of the Grand Lodge of Canada in the Province of Ontario.

Shortly after finishing his two-year term as Grand Master of the Grand Lodge of Canada in the Province of Ontario in July 1967, James Allan ran for re-election to the Legislature of Ontario for the riding of Haldimand-Norfolk as well as again in the fall of 1967 and 1971 and then again in 1975, at the age of almost 81, when James Allan lost to the Liberal candidate, Gordon Miller of Jarvis.

However, a year after stepping down as Grand Master, in 1968 James Allan stepped down from the Robarts' cabinet altogether and, through hindsight, one can see that the brilliant career of James Allan, successful businessman, municipal and provincial politician, high-ranking cabinet minister, friend, mentor and advisor to Premiers and a well-known, beloved, respected and high-ranking Mason, was beginning to wind down.

However, the seemingly boundless energy of James Allen was simply being re-directed towards other targets.

CHAPTER 12

THE BACKBENCHER ... AGAIN

IT IS 1968, AND IT HAS BEEN A YEAR SINCE JAMES ALLAN FINISHED HIS TWO-YEAR TERM AS Grand Master of the Grand Lodge of Canada in the Province of Ontario.

However, just because you have finished your term as Grand Master, Masonry does not allow Past Grand Masters to "fade away" into retirement or obscurity. Grand Lodge has a habit of keeping their Past Grand Masters busy.

As well, James had made the decision to step down as a cabinet minister in John Robarts' government, but was staying on as a backbencher for John Robarts.

In 1968 James Allan was appointed as the Chairman of the Niagara Parks Commission.

The Niagara Parks Commission had been created in 1885 and is responsible for just over 16 square kilometres of parkland along the Niagara River. In addition to this acreage, the

Commission is in charge of the Niagara Parkway, which winds 56 kilometres throughout the Niagara Falls and Niagara River area. In this corridor, the Commission manages the numerous trails, historic sites, picnic areas, and Commission attractions. These attractions include the Journey Behind the Falls, the Niagara Parks Butterfly Conservatory, and the Queenston Floral Clock. The Commission also manages the Navy Island National Historic Site under a lease agreement with the Parks Canada. It also owns the Chippewa Battlefield Park. The Commission has also developed a historical interpretive walk at this War of 1812 site. The Commission also operates the Botanical Gardens and since 1997, the Butterfly Conservatory.[17]

The Commission operates as well the Niagara Parks School of Horticulture, a world-renowned training centre for horticulturalists and gardeners.[17]

As Chair of the Niagara Parks Commission, James Allan took to his exceptional leadership and interpersonal skills along with his well-known drive and verve to the Commission.

Harry Bartlett recalled to me that, when James took over as Chairman of the Niagara Parks Commission, his first act were to "clean house" by letting all of the NPC's Commissioners go and putting new people in place.

For the next 20 years, James oversaw the Niagara Parks Commission not only continued to preserve and maintain what the Commission already possessed, but also directed an aggressive campaign of expansion, beautification and preservation of the Commission's holdings. The Niagara Parks Commission became one James Allan's most passionate undertakings.

Another target of James Allan's interest was the continued development of the Simcoe campus of Fanshawe College.

James was such an active patron and supporter of Fanshawe College that the Director of Fanshawe College named the James N. Allan Campus in 1988.

Even as a backbench MPP, James was highly respected, not just within the Progressive Conservative cabinet and caucus, but James also received the same respect and admiration from the Her Majesty's Loyal Opposition, the Liberal Part of Ontario as well the caucus of the New Democratic Party.

When James spoke, both sides of the Legislature, government and opposition, listened. No one dared jeer, sneer or make snide remarks like which is done now.

Premier Davis related to me that James, even as a backbencher, was the driving force to change the legislation that governed the school boards registration, moving the registration from the township/school section era to the new epoch of school districts and registrations being drawn around existing county boundaries.

As always, James continued to do what he did better than anyone else, his constituency work, and he maintained his reputation for doing it well. James' riding, Haldimand-Norfolk, stretched from Lowbanks, ON, some 40 kilometres south south-east of Dunnville, ON west to the outskirts of Tillsonburg, ON, west of Courtland, ON. A total distance of some 110 kilometres, or just short of 70 miles.

North from Port Dover, on to Caledonia, ON, as distance of almost 50 kilometres or just over 30 miles. Haldimand-Norfolk was, and still is a very large and diverse riding, both in terms of economics and demographics.

However, as stated many times in this volume, constituency work was the hallmark of James' 24 year tenure as the MPP for Haldimand-Norfolk.

James would consistently appear at many functions he was made aware of, perhaps an opening of a new wing or program at the Simcoe Research Station on behalf of the Ministry of Agriculture, or at Fanshawe College in Simcoe, which campus bears his name. Or perhaps he would attend at a Junior Farmer banquet in either, or both, Haldimand or Norfolk Counties, or maybe at someone's silver or golden wedding anniversary.

Sometimes there would be several events in just one day.

However, what sets James Allan apart from the MPP's and MP's of today's society is James, when he arrived, would talk with everyone at whatever the function may be or wherever it was held. He would not leave until he spoke with everyone.

While people or news reporters would be there to take photographs and interview James, he would not bolt for the doors once the "photo-op" was complete, unlike the MPP's and MP's of today.

Harry Bartlett said that James Allan liked to think of himself just as a "common" man, who related well to the voters of Haldimand-Norfolk. James' level of communication was legendary, unlike today when most times it is well-nigh impossible to get your MPP or MP on the telephone, let alone speak to you, even to say "hello."

James Allan knew the voters relied on him and James never forgot that. For nearly 60 years, those voters remembered James' at the ballot box.

CHAPTER 13

TIME TO RETIRE...REALLY

IT IS FALL 1971 AND JAMES ALLAN HAS WON HIS SIXTH CONSECUTIVE PROVINCIAL ELECTION as the MPP for Haldimand-Norfolk. James has been a backbench MPP for the past three years after stepping down from John Robarts' cabinet.

There is a new Premier in Ontario, William Davis, James' former cabinet colleague, who had won the Ontario Progressive Conservative leadership race in March, 1971 after John Robarts had retired. Premier Davis would rely heavily upon his former cabinet and caucus colleague for advice and direction once again.

Premier Davis has many plans for Ontario, and some destined to become not so popular.

Two of those initiatives announced in 1972 were to bring in a new type of governance for some municipalities in Ontario called "regional government." Two of the municipalities in

Ontario that would be severely affected were Haldimand and Norfolk Counties.

In Ontario, regional municipalities were created to provide common services to urban and rural municipalities in the way that counties typically provide common services to rural municipalities. Only certain predominantly urban divisions are given the status of a regional municipality in Ontario; most census divisions instead retain the status of a county or a district.

The specific relationship of a regional government and the cities, towns, townships and villages within its borders is determined by provincial legislation; typically the regional municipality provides many core services such as police protection, waste management and in some, public transit. Similar to counties, they also provide infrastructure for main roads, sewers, and bridges and also handle social services. Organization of regional government has occasionally been controversial, as council membership was, at times, determined by the constituent municipalities rather than elected directly.[17]

In 1971, the Province of Ontario announced that municipalities that made up Ottawa, Sudbury, Hamilton, Burlington, St. Catharines and the Niagara area and their surrounding areas, along with Haldimand and Norfolk Counties were going to be converted from the County/Township system to regional municipalities.

The other initiative was the announcement of the province's intention to build two "satellite" communities in Haldimand and Norfolk Counties, one in South Cayuga Township and the other in the north-west corner of Walpole Township and south-east corner of Norfolk County's Townsend Township, called "Townsend." The Treasurer in the Davis cabinet at that time, John White, confidently predicted that 100 000 people would call the proposed satellite city in Townsend itself home by 1990.

The "satellite city" called Townsend has, in 2016, about 900 residents and has never been above a population of 1 000 residents, let alone 100 000 inhabitants.

This population explosion was to have been caused by the industrial and commercial expansion at the Nanticoke Industrial Park south-east of Jarvis in Walpole Township. In the late 1960's and early 1970's, Stelco had committed to this area by building a new, state-of-the-art steel mill, along with Texaco establishing an oil refinery and Ontario Hydro constructing a new thermal generating station.

When the Ontario government's real estate people starting going around to various farms and other properties in Haldimand County's South Cayuga and Walpole Townships and Norfolk County's Townsend Township, purchasing and assembling land for these proposed satellite communities, problems stated to surface with disparities in what the government's real estate agents were paying to some landowners and what those same agents were paying to others.

Please realize that even if the government had included in some sales agreements a "non-disclosure" clause preventing some landowners from discussing what the government paid them for their land, these land sales, when closed, had to be registered at the Land Registry Offices in either Haldimand County in Cayuga or Norfolk County in Simcoe.

Any information registered with either of those Land Registry Offices is considered public information and accessible by anyone. When the author operated his law practice, he upset and annoyed many people by being able to access information about their properties, homes, what they had paid for them or what they sold for, as these people mistakenly considered information such as this as private information and not available to just anyone.

So it is no small wonder that some landowners would find out that some other property-owners got more money per acre than someone else.

As well, many of the residents in both Haldimand and Norfolk Counties were not at all enamoured at having regional government forced down their throats. Many did not want to lose all the historical connections built up from nearly 125 years of service, or their system of municipal government taken away that was felt had served Haldimand and Norfolk Counties well, and would have preferred to continue the status quo.

As well, in the early 1970's, after many years of economic growth and prosperity in Ontario, the economy, not just in Ontario but for most of Canada began to stagnate and go into a recession along with suffering from severe inflation. The state of the economy had been further exacerbated by the Arab oil embargo of late 1973. These sorts of situations of course spell electoral trouble for any sitting provincial or federal government. As stated earlier, voters are known to take their frustrations out on whatever government happens to be in the way.

It is the summer of 1975, and Bill Davis calls a provincial election for 18 September 1975. Davis is running on his record from the previous four years, but the Ontario electorate was in a sour and very foul mood, and Haldimand-Norfolk was no exception to this situation.

The combined issues of the economy, regional government and the satellite cities have combined for a "perfect storm" in an electoral sense.

The Liberal Party of Ontario has running as a candidate in Haldimand-Norfolk a well-known Jarvis-area farmer, Gordon Miller who has a wealth of local political experience. Gordon Miller was also known locally for selling a large swath of his farm and property to the Ontario government for the satellite city at Townsend.

However, the electorate in Haldimand-Norfolk was what could be considered ugly and voters, not just in Haldimand-Norfolk but across Ontario, were ready for a change.

On 18 September 1975, the Progressive Conservative government of Bill Davis was reduced by 27 seats, from a 78-seat majority government to a 51-seat minority government, the first time in more than 30 years that the Progressive Conservatives faced a minority government circumstance.

However, one of those 27 Progressive Conservative seats that was lost was James Allan's long-held seat in Haldimand-Norfolk as James went down to defeat at the hands of Gordon Miller of the Liberal Party of Ontario.

The defeat of James Allan bought an end to a long and storied political career, both municipal and provincial, that had spanned some 60 years. James Allan had won countless municipal elections and was elected six times to Queen's Park, all consecutively since 1915.

James Allan had become a household name, not to just one generation, but to several generations. James had been a major part of, and reason for Ontario's rapid and continued growth after World War II.

As well, James Allan had been responsible for such massive undertakings such as the Burlington Bay Skyway and the initial introduction of the Ontario Retail Sales Tax, or "Frostbite." James was also the steadying hand at Ontario's fiscal tiller for eight years and was the last Ontario Treasurer to report a budgetary surplus for 30 years.

While many of us, this author included, may not have always agreed with the politics of James Noble Allan, one can never quarrel the fact that with James Allan, after God, his church and his family, his constituents in Haldimand-Norfolk always came first and the rest of Ontario came in a close second.

James Allan took pride in his constituency work and voters repaid James' pride in them by giving James their confidence and an incredible run of electoral victories in both the municipal and provincial spectrum. And it is very unlikely you will ever see anyone construct such a run of municipal and provincial electoral successes ever again.

What is most unfortunate is that the breed of politician that James Allan was has now become all but extinct. Our politicians now in Haldimand-Norfolk, most notably in the provincial and federal spectrum, are only concerned with assisting constituents from their own party and getting their picture in the local newspapers as much as possible - especially in an election year.

If you had the colossal nerve to not vote for them and you need help...well, you can likely go pound salt. The author knows this from personal experience.

In this day and age, we desperately need another James Allan to assist us and serve us, not the motley group of parliamentarians we have now been saddled with for nearly a generation.

CHAPTER 14

RIDING OFF INTO THE SUNSET

IT IS NOW FALL 1975, AND JAMES ALLAN FAST APPROACHING 81 YEARS OF AGE. JAMES HAS already been collecting his CPP pension since its inception in 1965. As well, with James' electoral defeat a by Gordon Miller in the 1975 provincial election, he is eligible for a parliamentary severance package along with a pension based on his 24 years of service in the Ontario Legislature.

However, when one considers what James Noble Allan had done over the course of his 73-year career in politics for Canborough Township, the Town of Dunnville, for Haldimand County, for the Province of Ontario and the Niagara Parks Commission, no one would begrudge whatever parliamentary pension and severance package James was entitled to.

James Allan was a rarity; he was a politician who was worth what he was paid. Perhaps he was worth more than he was paid. To those of us that knew him, perchance yes.

James Allan was one of the very few, perhaps the only, politician in the country who deserved every penny he got in a severance or a pension. Perhaps even more, James Allan was that valuable.

While James no longer was the MPP for Haldimand-Norfolk, he did continue on as the Chairman of the Niagara Parks Commission for another 13 years. James Allan was not fully retired until 1988, when James was almost 94 years old.

Robert Nixon related to this author when he was campaigning door-to-door in Dunnville prior to the September 1991 provincial election. Bob was walking along a quiet residential street in Dunnville in late August or early September 1991. He went on to recount that he spied a familiar-looking older gentleman raking his lawn and he approached him.

Of course the man raking his lawn was the almost-97 year old James Allan. Bob stated that they had quite a long conversation with each other, and finally James advised Bob, somewhat "tongue in cheek," that "You know Bob, I really can't vote for you. I hope you realize that." Bob stated that they had a good laugh, shook hands and parted ways.

Bob related to me that it was less than a year later when he found out that James had been admitted into the Haldimand War Memorial Hospital in Dunnville, Bob had a final visit with James shortly before James Allan passed away in May 1992.

As well, Darcy McKeough imparted to this author that the last time he met James was at the funeral of James' wife in 1986, Lillian, and said that James was still keen and sharp, and James knew everybody who came into the funeral home.

While James Allan knew everyone in Dunnville, and everyone knew him, James was able to live out his well-earned retirement in relative quietude and obscurity.

Of course, while life is many things, it is not eternal. As the comedian George Carlin once panned, *"While God is great, everything he creates, dies. No one gets out of this life alive."*

With James being a Mason, when he would pass to the Grand Lodge Above, there would be, in addition to the customary wake and funeral, a Masonic Memorial Service which would be hosted by James' mother Lodge, Amity Lodge #32 in Dunnville.

When this author first announced at Amity Lodge in the fall of 2010 that he was starting to research and to write this book, Amity members such as V. W. Bro. John Chapman, V. W. Bro. Michael Palmer and R. W. Bro Paul Shaver all related to the author of their own fears, concerns and anxieties, and of the other Amity brethren who were working their way through the officer's chairs at Amity Lodge on their way to becoming a Worshipful Masters of Amity Lodge #32 during the time through the late 1980's through the early 1990's.

Every Worshipful Master during that time realized that, if the M. W. Bro. James Allan passed away on their "Masonic watch," they would have the Masonic Memorial Service to assist in planning, to organize and in arranging. They would also be greeting the multitudes of individuals paying their respects.

Everyone knew that both the Masonic Memorial Service and the funeral of M. W. Bro. James Allan would be an incredibly colossal affair, attended by hundreds, if not several thousand or more people. Various present and past Grand Lodge officers, fellow Masons, federal, provincial and municipal politicians and parliamentarians, and not just the many residents of Dunnville and Haldimand County, but from all over Ontario, Canada and the United States, people would congregate on Dunnville to pay their respects to James Allan and his family.

Talk about performing on a "grand" stage. These Amity brethren shuddered at the thought of not just attending this Masonic Memorial Service, but assisting in carrying off the service without making any mistakes. Those thoughts would be terrifying.

On Saturday, 9 May 1992, the inevitable occurred. At the Haldimand War Memorial Hospital in Dunnville, a hospital that James Allan was instrumental in creating and which James was a proud patron of, our M. W. Bro. James Noble Allan passed to the Grand Lodge Above, almost 74 years a Mason.

I spoke with R. W. Bro. Paul Shaver, who was Worshipful Master of Amity Lodge #32 for the first time in 1992 and would have been responsible for assisting Grand Lodge with the Masonic Memorial Service for M. W. Bro. James Allan. However, R. W. Bro. Shaver stated that he was out of town for reasons of employment at the time of M. W. Bro. James Allan's passing.

So the task of assisting Grand Lodge with the Masonic Memorial Service fell to the Senior Warden at the time, V. W. Bro. Michael Palmer.

V. W. Bro. Palmer related to this author that the Grand Master of the day, our M. W. Bro. Norman E. Byrne and Grand Lodge had looked after the vast majority of the planning and the arrangements for the Masonic Memorial Service and the officers and members of Amity Lodge #32 were called upon when necessary for any facilitation or roles with the Masonic Memorial Service.

Some two months later, at the Annual Communication of the Grand lodge of Canada in the Province of Ontario on 15 & 16 July 1992, in the Grand Master's Address to the brethren of the Grand Lodge of Canada in the Province of Ontario, the

Grand Master, M. W. Bro, Norman E. Byrne paid homage to the recently-departed M. W. Bro. James N. Allan with the following homily:[19]

> *"M.W. Bro. James Allan hailed from the Dunnville area of our province and it was there that he entered the dairy business in 1919. Jim Allan was an active and benevolent member and a life elder of Grace United Church which he served for a lifetime. Bro. Allan's public service began with municipal councils at Canboro and at Dunnville. He served Dunnville as mayor and was a past warden of the then County of Haldimand. He entered provincial affairs in 1951 when he was elected a member of the Ontario legislature as member for Haldimand-Norfolk. He soon became a member of cabinet and was appointed Treasurer of Ontario in 1958, a position he held with dignity for many years.*

> *In Masonry, our distinguished brother was initiated into the craft in Amity Lodge No. 32, at Dunnville, and remained an active member of that lodge until his death. He served his Mother Lodge as Worshipful Master in 1925 and shortly thereafter was elected D.D.G.M. of Niagara District "A". In 1947 he joined the Board of General Purposes of Grand Lodge and served it well and actively until he was elected D.G.M. in 1963. In July of 1965 he ascended the Chair of the Royal Solomon as Grand Master. M.W. Bro. Allan carried his skill and activity into many branches of Masonry.*

He was a Royal Arch Mason, a Scottish Riter and was made an Honorary 33° Mason in 1961. He was invited to join the Royal Order of Scotland in 1963 and was a life member of Rameses Temple of the Shrine. During his years of service to our Grand Lodge, he contributed a great deal and was instrumental in providing a long term and excellent tenant for our Grand Lodge building. His wise counsel, care and concern for all persons with whom he came into contact will be sadly missed by a host of friends and admirers in the craft, in the community and in government circles. He was highly respected by members of all political parties in Ontario as witness the attendance by many of his political opponents at his funeral service.

Anyone who had the opportunity of knowing M.W. Bro. James Allan will find it difficult to fill the void his death has caused. We shall miss him."

V. W. Bro. Michael Palmer did relate to this author that the day of the Masonic Memorial Service, the Grand Master, the various Grand Lodge officers and Amity officers were sequestered at one point in the Amity Lodge room in order to facilitate the arrangements of Masonic Memorial Service. One of the politicians of the day who attended was the former Premier of Ontario, Michael Harris. In 1992, Michael Harris was the Leader of the Ontario Progressive Conservative Party.

Michael Harris wanted to be included in the private meeting of Grand Lodge officers and others in the Amity Lodge room. However, as Michael Harris was not a Mason, he was not allowed in. This author was advised that Mr. Harris was not happy at being excluded from this meeting.

The day of James Allan's funeral, Tuesday, 12 May 1992, was a beautiful day, a great day for everyone and anyone to bid farewell to not only a great Mason, but to a man who dedicated two-thirds of his life to public service.

Not only did Haldimand County benefit greatly from the presence of James Allan, so did the Province of Ontario.

While Haldimand County and the Province of Ontario has long profited from the long shadow and legacy of James Allan, it could be said there would not be enough time, or sufficient ways, in the world to say "thank you" enough to James Allan.

One has to look very far and very wide to find another person of the stature of James Noble Allan.

CHAPTER 15

EPILOGUE

AN OFTEN USED, PERHAPS INORDINATELY OVER-USED AND UNDENIABLY WELL-WORN PHRASE that is many times oft-quoted when someone who is famous (or infamous) or who is very well-known passes on is that their demise "is the end of an era."

However, in the words of that immortal bard, *"There was ne'er a truer word spoken"*[20] when one thinks of James Noble Allan.

Conversely, in this instance the passing of James Noble Allan was many things to many people. He was a loved son, a sibling, a beloved husband, a father, an adored grandfather, a great-grandfather, a farmer, a shrewd businessman, an astute municipal politician, a perspicacious provincial parliamentarian, a sage cabinet minister, a respected brother Mason and most of all, a very quiet, soft-spoken, but very true and towering leader.

There are those of us who are old enough and were able to know and are fortunate enough to fondly remember James

Noble Allan. There are very, very few of us around anymore that do clearly remember James Noble Allan. So when one does think of James Noble Allan, we think of just plain "Jim," of his simplicity and his immense integrity. We think of his dedication to the people of Ontario. Every time we cross the Burlington Bay, James N. Allan Skyway we evoke his legacy. We think of and we remember the man, Mason and the MPP, we think of a man who unhesitatingly, unflinchingly and unselfishly devoted some 73 years, three-quarters of his life to public service.

For 73 years, from 1915 all the way through to 1988, through the Great War, the Great Depression, World War II, incredible economic growth and prosperity as well as some economic turbulence for Ontario, James Noble Allan represented his various constituents, their interests and was at the forefront of Canborough Township, the Town of Dunnville, Haldimand County, and later the Ontario government, then onto chairing the Niagara Parks Commission. He was often at the tiller, assisting in first leading and blazing a trail for Haldimand County, then skilfully steering and guiding that vessel known as the Province of Ontario through the maze of economic growth, avoiding any dangers or pitfalls.

It was the foresight, the drive and the vision of James Allan that brought us the Burlington Bay Skyway.

Where would the industrial engine of Ontario be, or the QEW, and Ontario in general, not to mention traffic congestion, without the Burlington Bay Skyway? Quite likely not where it is now.

Also, could the Province of Ontario have afforded its various health, education, transportation and other economic programs without the revenue from the Ontario Retail Sales Tax? A deficit would have been more likely.

Without the Ontario Retail Sales Tax, it is quite possible that Ontario would likely rank near the bottom of the health care ratings along with have-not jurisdictions like Alabama and Mississippi without the foresight, the drive and leadership of James Noble Allan.

Could the Progressive Conservative political dynasty that governed Ontario from 1943 to 1985 and commanded by the likes of Thomas Kennedy, George Drew, Leslie Frost, John Robarts and Bill Davis indeed have survived those 42 years without James Noble Allan and his steady leadership, wise counsel, his sage stewardship and great popularity? Perhaps, but not without finding someone else taking the place of James Allan.

That task alone would be gargantuan.

The late R. W. Bro. Harry Bartlett stated to this author that James Noble Allan not only did a great deal for Masonry in Ontario, but also for Amity Lodge, for Canborough Township, for Dunnville, for Haldimand County and for the Province of Ontario.

A person in the form of James Noble Allan does not come along very often. Certainly not every year, decade or even in a generation, or even two or three generations. Maybe once in a century, if we are lucky.

We desperately need again the leadership and guidance of someone of the ilk of James Noble Allan. A parliamentarian who looks after ALL of his constituents. Not just his friends, his cronies or only those people who voted for him and pretending the rest do not exist. We need a person who has the good of ALL of the public at large, always in the forefront of his mind, not just too only get their name and picture in the local newspapers as much as possible while doing little else.

Ontario and its residents need the vision, courage, audacity and leadership of a James Allan once again. Ontario needs someone who has the courage of their convictions to draft, table, move forward and advocate for the necessary legislation that will put Ontario back on the right track to more and better prosperity. Someone is needed who will not just scratch the surface of some contentious issue while ignoring the "elephant in the room," and hoping it will go away if you do not acknowledge it.

The populace of Ontario should be eternally indebted and express gratitude to the Great Architect of the Universe for being blessed with the very long shadow and the leviathan of a presence of, as well as the legacy and the length of time we enjoyed James Noble Allan and his benefits, qualities and his many worthy attributes.

Ontario needs another James Noble Allan and Ontario very much needs him now.

As always, hope springs eternal.

So mote it be.

W. Bro. Allison Gowling
Jarvis, ON
June 2016

CHAPTER 16

A BRIEF BIOGRAPHY OF OUR GRAND MASTER

EXERTED FROM THE GRAND LODGE PROCEEDINGS, 1965 [19]

"James Noble Allan was born in the Township of Canboro in the County of Haldimand, about seven miles from Dunnville. His first school in Canboro was not far from his father's home. It was one of those seats of learning, which, over the early years of the century, produced great men. He entered the Ontario Agricultural College at Guelph from which he graduated in 1914 with the degree of B.S.A. On graduation he returned to the family farm where he continued his occupation as a farmer. During the next five years, in addition to farming, he was periodically Agricultural Representative in

the Counties of Lanark and Wentworth. While at College in Guelph he met Lilian Harvie, then a student at Macdonald Institute in the same city. After each had graduated they married. They have two children, a son and daughter, both married. They also have eight grandchildren.

In 1919 he entered the Dairy business in Dunnville, which business he personally carried on for many years; this operation is still carried on by the family.

He is a member and life Elder of Grace United Church, Dunnville. He has been a member of The Lions Club of Dunnville for more than thirty years.

His public service began with Municipal Councils in the Township of Canboro and in the Town of Dunnville. He served in the Dunnville Town Council and the Haldimand County Council for nineteen years. He is a former Mayor of Dunnville and a past Warden of the County of Haldimand. During these years he became President of The Good Roads Association of Ontario and is now an Honourary Member of that Association. He is also an Honourary Member of the Canadian Good Roads Association.

He entered Provincial affairs in 1951 when he was elected to the Provincial Legislature as Member for Haldimand-Norfolk. In January, 1955, he became a Member of the Provincial Cabinet and first administered the portfolio of Highways. He has held a total of five portfolios. In 1958 he was appointed Treasurer of the Province of Ontario, a position which he still holds.

He was initiated in Amity Lodge, A.F. & A.M., No. 32. Dunnville, in 1919 and was Worshipful Master of his Mother Lodge in 1925. In 1931 he was elected District Deputy Grand Master of Niagara "A" District. In 1947 and 1949 he was appointed to the Board of General Purposes of Grand Lodge. In 1951 he was elected to that Board and was re-elected each alternate year to and including the year of 1961. In 1963 he was elected Deputy Grand Master and was installed as Grand Master in July, 1965.

He is a member of McCallum Chapter, Royal Arch Masons, Dunnville. He is also a member of Murton Lodge of Perfection, the Hamilton Sovereign Chapter of Rose Croix, and the Moore Sovereign Consistory. Ancient and Accepted Scottish Rite of

Canada. He was received into the Provincial Grand Lodge of the Royal Order of Scotland in 1963. In September, 1961, he was coroneted as Honourary Inspector-General of the Supreme Council A. And A.S. Rite, 33°. He is a life member of the Ancient and Arabic Order Nobles of the Mystic Shrine Rameses Temple, Toronto.

In the spring of 1961 he was awarded the degree of Doctor of Laws, Honouris Causa, by McMaster University, Hamilton.

An honour of a different type is his membership in the Mohawk Tribe of Six Nations Indians as Honourary Chief. He is known as "Ga-nedas", meaning "Tall Pine".

For more than fifty years he has been known to everyone as just plain "Jim".

As the Most Worshipful, the Grand Master, he will preside at meetings of the Grand Lodge with dignity and will ever maintain the present prestige of that high office."

BIBLIOGRAPHY & REFERENCES

1. Ch. 1; Haldimand County Atlas, H. R. Page & Co., 1879;

2. Ch. 3; National Bureau of Economic Research, 1909-1919;

3. Ch. 3; University of Guelph Archival and Special Collections Department;

4. Ch. 3; Interview of James N. Allan by N. R. Richards, University of Guelph, 1987;

5. Ch. 4; Dunnville District Heritage Association, the Late Lorne Sorge and "Remember When," Vol. #3;

6. Ch. 4; The Orillia Packet, 16 July 1916, Family of Gwen David Cunningham & Dale Cunningham - Person Sheet 29 April 2015;

7. Ch. 6; Caledonia Opera House Fire, Wikipedia;

8. Ch. 7; James Noble Allan, Wikipedia 2015;

9. Ch. 8; Burlington Bay Skyway, Wikipedia 2015;

10. Ch. 11; Grand Lodge Proceedings, 1947;

11. Ch. 11; Grand Lodge Proceedings, 1949:

12. Ch. 11; Grand Lodge Proceedings, 1951:

13. Ch. 11; Grand Lodge Proceedings, 1919 – 1992;

14. Ch. 11; Grand Lodge Proceedings, 1966 & 1967;

15. Ch. 11; Grand Lodge Proceedings, 1966;

16. Ch. 11; Grand Lodge Proceedings, 1966;

17. Ch. 12; Niagara Parks Commission, Wikipedia, 2015;

18. Ch. 13; Definition of regional munici-
    palities, Wikipedia, 2015;

19. Ch. 14; Grand Lodge Proceedings, 1992;

20. Ch. 15; William Shakespeare (but
    you knew that...didn't you? ;)

21. Ch. 16; Grand Lodge Proceedings, 1965.

ABOUT THE AUTHOR

ALLISON GOWLING IS A NATIVE OF HALDIMAND COUNTY, WHO WAS BORN ON HIS PARENTS' dairy farm in May 1957. Allison's father, Norman was a well-known dairy farmer, Holstein breeder and also a Mason and a Past Master (1965) of St. John's Lodge #35 in Cayuga.

Allison's Mother, Ethel was a well-recognized and fondly remembered elementary school teacher who taught in many one-room schoolhouses in and around Haldimand County as well as supply teaching for many years. There are still a few of her former students still around Haldimand County that recall Ethel's teaching abilities as well as her quick hand at classroom discipline.

Allison attended elementary school in Cayuga at J. L. Mitchener in Cayuga, and also Seneca Central in the suburbs of Empire Corners and Cayuga Secondary School.

After graduation, Allison worked at the Hamilton Street Railway until suffering a partially disabling spinal injury in 1993 and was offered the opportunity to undergo vocational retraining by the Workers' Compensation Board and attended

Sheridan College in Brampton. There Allison undertook the two-year Court & Tribunal Program, graduating in 1997 fifth in his class with a 3.72 GPA.

After graduation, Allison operated a professional law practice in Haldimand County for 13 years, becoming a regular fixture at many local, and some not-so-local courthouses, and is now embarking on a new career as a writer.

Allison has always had a keen interest in history, especially local history and is considered well-informed and knowledgeable on the history of Haldimand County. With Allison's being fifth generation on his father's side who emigrated in 1843 after assisting David Thompson with the design and construction of the Grand River Navigation Company's series of locks and dams between 1820 and 1829. On his mother's side, Allison is a sixth generation United Empire Loyalist. Allison has been extremely fortunate to not only have been a witness to history in his time, but also being able to learn about local history, not only at his parents' knee, but on the knees of Allison's numerous relatives (I mean he has a LOT of relatives...you cannot keep their names straight without a program!).

In 1999, Allison was initiated, passed and raised into Masonry at St. Andrew's Masonic Lodge #62 and was Worshipful Master at St. Andrew's in 2006. Since then, Allison has served on several District teams, the Craft Association of the Hamilton Districts, the Masonic Past Masters' Association of the Hamilton Districts and the Grand Lodge Library Committee. Allison is also a member of the Murton Lodge of Perfection, the Sovereign Chapter of Rose Croix and the Moore Sovereign Consistory at the Scottish Rite in Hamilton.

Allison is currently a member of Hillcrest Lodge, #594 in Hamilton.

In 1981, Allison married Annemiek Lavertu of Cayuga, who is currently employed at the Brantford Public Library as a Circulation Clerk, and they have resided in Haldimand County since then and in Jarvis for nearly 30 years. They have two adult sons, Gregory and Kyle, both who have joined their father in the Craft.

CPSIA information can be obtained
at www.ICGtesting.com
Printed in the USA
LVOW11s0012031216
515425LV00004B/4/P